PAPERCRAFTS

PAPERCRAFTS

50 Extraordinary Gifts and Projects, Step by Step

Gillian Souter

CROWN TRADE PAPERBACKS

New York

Published by Crown Trade Paperbacks, 201 East 50th Street, New York, New York 10022. Member of the Crown Publishing Group.

Random House, Inc. New York, Toronto, London, Sydney, Auckland

CROWN TRADE PAPBERBACKS and colophon are trademarks of Crown Publishers, Inc.

Originally published in Australia by Off the Shelf Publishing in 1994.

Manufactured in Hong Kong

LIBRARY OF CONGRESS CATALOGING-IN-PUBLICATION DATA

Souter, Gillian
Papercrafts: 50 extraordinary gifts and projects, step-by-step /
Gillian Souter.
        p. cm.
Originally published: Lewisham, NSW: Off the Shelf Pub., 1994.
Includes index.
1. Paper work. 2. Paper toy making. I. Title.
TT870.S67 1995
745.54—dc20   95-12995
                                               CIP
ISBN 0-517-88484-4

10 9 8 7 6 5 4 3 2 1

First American Edition

Foreword

Some people like the feel of clay under the fingernails. Others enjoy the tension of yarn on the knitting needles. There is little, though, to surpass the different sensations offered by papercrafts: the rough deckled edge of handmade paper, the crisp lines of sculptured card, the firm spring of a quilled coil.

Those new to the pleasures of working with paper will discover much in this book to whet their appetites. It introduces methods of making paper, cutting it up, decorating it and shaping it. Specific topics range from the ancient skills of weaving and relief printing to the delicate arts of découpage and embossing. For each method, you'll find a detailed overview along with three imaginative projects, including:

A personal item, ideal as a gift

Something useful for the home

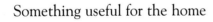

A toy or game for the young
(or the young at heart)

As well, there are ideas for wrapping presents and tips on making boxes and gift tags because, in addition to the pleasures of the papercrafts themselves, there is the joy of giving your work to someone special.

Contents

Paper

Paper is essentially a sheet of intertwined fibers. However, it can be produced with such variation that it sometimes doesn't seem like the same material. The main variables are the type of fiber, their arrangement, the paper's weight and the coating.

The longer the fibers, the stronger the paper. Most paper today is made with short wood fibers. If the fibers lie in the same direction, as happens during mass-production, a grain direction is created. Paper will fold and tear more easily along the grain. It will also swell sideways when painted or glued. Always determine the grain direction of the paper you are using and be aware of it when planning a project (see page 12).

The weight of paper affects its flexibility. Heavy paper is referred to as card and will prove less flexible when you try to roll it. Sheets of card are sometimes laminated together to form board.

When it is formed, paper has a natural matt surface and is quite absorbent. It is usually coated or "sized" with a glue-like substance to give it a glossy surface and to prevent inks or paints from seeping when used on it. It is possible to buy unsized paper.

Different methods of production result in specific features. Handmade paper, formed on a mold and deckle, has four deckle edges and no grain direction. Machine-made paper does have a definite grain and is often heavily sized. Mold-made paper shares some of the qualities of the other two. It has a grain direction but has two deckle edges and may have long fibers.

Throughout this book, different papers have been used in the projects and also as backgrounds in the photographs. It is worthwhile investing in an array of papers so that you can experiment with different textures and colors.

Handmade paper has a deckle edge and natural irregularities.

Japanese papers are absorbent and contain very long fibers.

Some papers are printed with a subtle pattern, making them ideal for stationery or backgrounds.

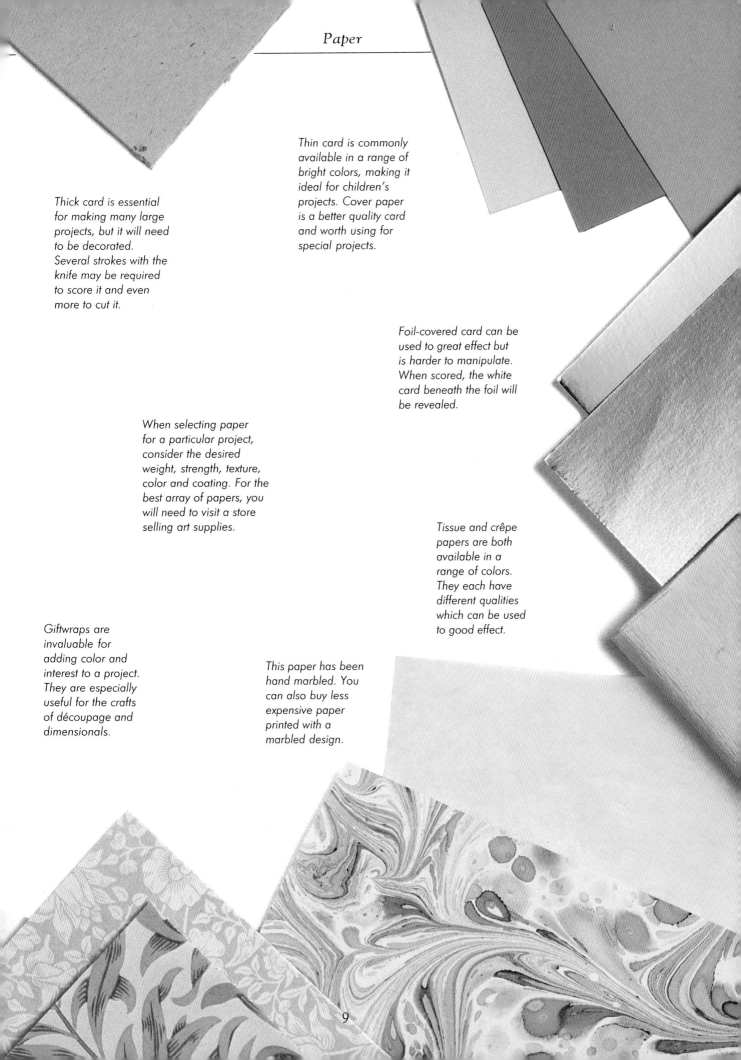

Thin card is commonly available in a range of bright colors, making it ideal for children's projects. Cover paper is a better quality card and worth using for special projects.

Thick card is essential for making many large projects, but it will need to be decorated. Several strokes with the knife may be required to score it and even more to cut it.

Foil-covered card can be used to great effect but is harder to manipulate. When scored, the white card beneath the foil will be revealed.

When selecting paper for a particular project, consider the desired weight, strength, texture, color and coating. For the best array of papers, you will need to visit a store selling art supplies.

Tissue and crêpe papers are both available in a range of colors. They each have different qualities which can be used to good effect.

Giftwraps are invaluable for adding color and interest to a project. They are especially useful for the crafts of découpage and dimensionals.

This paper has been hand marbled. You can also buy less expensive paper printed with a marbled design.

Equipment

Unlike many other crafts, papercraft does not usually require a vast array of expensive and specialized equipment. However, having a wider selection of tools does allow you to choose the perfect one for each task and good quality equipment makes the craft even more enjoyable.

A craft knife with a retractable and replaceable blade is essential, although some craftspeople also use a scalpel which has a very fine blade. Scissors are sometimes needed as well: keep one pair for cutting paper and another for cutting tape. A self-healing cutting mat, which is often marked with useful guidelines, is also necessary. Use a metal ruler for ruling and cutting straight lines, as plastic or wooden rulers are easily damaged. Graphite pencils and a good eraser, such as a kneadable one, are invaluable. A bone paper-folder is a small luxury which is wonderful for smoothly creasing folds and scores.

Specific types of papercraft may require a few extra tools: these are explained in the introduction to each chapter. Equipment and materials needed for each project are listed in a box above the project picture.

Counterclockwise: a scalpel; a craft knife; curved scissors; a cutting mat and tracing paper; a circle template; a small and large metal ruler.

Clockwise:
a roller; fast-drying
glue; white glue;
a bone folder;
double-sided tape;
clear adhesive tape;
a graphite pencil;
a compass;
a kneadable eraser;
a hole punch.

Basic Techniques

The techniques used in papercraft are so fundamental that many will seem like second nature. Indeed, most of them were probably taught to you in your first few years at school. This isn't to say that they don't require skill. An accurate eye and a deft hand are essential if you want those clean, sharp lines that the best examples of papercraft exhibit.

One of the most important steps to achieving this is to handle the paper correctly. Store sheets of paper flat if possible. If you don't have room to do this, roll it very loosely. It should be kept in a dry place, out of direct sunlight. Make sure your hands are clean and dry before handling paper and lift large sheets by diagonally opposite corners so that they do not buckle.

Determine the grain direction of your paper by one of the two methods below. Remember that a fold along the grain direction will be sharper and a tear will be neater. This is especially important if, for example, your project involves a concertina or cylinder, or if you are tearing a paper appliqué design. When gluing two pieces of paper together, try to match the grain direction.

Some papercrafts require precise measurements and folds. Plot out shapes with pencil marks and lines before cutting them. Use a set square and protractor to check any important angles, especially when cutting box templates. A compass or circle template make it easier to draw perfect circles.

Finding the Grain

▶ *There are several ways to determine the grain direction of a sheet of paper. One technique is to place the sheet on a flat surface and roll one side to meet the other. Release it, then roll the bottom edge to meet the top; if there is less resistance this time, then the grain runs from side to side, otherwise it runs lengthwise.*

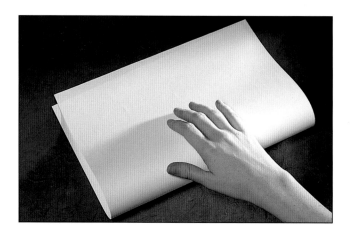

◄ *Another method of finding the grain direction, although this will damage the paper, is to tear one strip from across the sheet and another down. Tearing with the grain will result in a smoother edge, while it is harder to control a tear against the grain.*

Transferring Patterns

◄ *To transfer a pattern for a project, lay tracing paper on the book and trace over the lines in pencil. If the pattern is reversible (as most of them are) simply turn the tracing over, place it on the project paper and run the pencil over the lines. If it is not reversible, you will need to run a pencil over the reverse and then redraw over the first face.*

When transferring a pattern onto black or foil-covered card, use a knitting needle or ballpoint pen instead of a pencil to transfer from the tracing paper. This will make an impression in the card's surface which is easier to see than a pencil mark.

Scaling Patterns

► *Scaling or resizing a pattern is easy to do with the use of a photocopier. Alternatively, you can use the squaring up method. Trace the pattern and rule a ½ " grid over it. If the instructions specify to enlarge it by 200%, rule a 1 " grid on a fresh piece of tracing paper and copy the pattern square by square.*

Folding & Scoring

▶ Any dashed lines appearing in a pattern indicate a fold or a score. A scored line is one that is lightly drawn with a knife, merely breaking the top fibers and allowing the paper to fold more crisply. Some paper is too thin to be scored and should be merely folded.

Cutting

◀ Make sure your knife blade is sharp, replacing it when necessary. Cut with a firm action, ensuring that the paper fibers are not being dragged. Use a metal ruler for cutting straight lines. For curved lines, hold the knife as you would a pen, as in the picture on the left.

Using Adhesives

▶ Choose the most suitable adhesive material for each task. White glue can wrinkle thin papers. A strong, fast-drying glue may be needed to secure the sides of a large box. Double-sided tape is very useful for precise work. Spray adhesive is ideal for gluing large areas but should be used in a well-ventilated area.

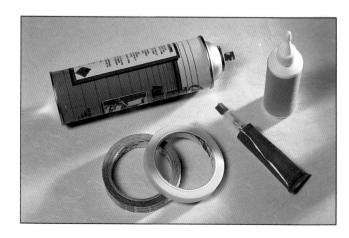

The Projects

To allow you to try out many different forms of papercraft, each technique chapter in this book contains three projects. These have been designed to demonstrate the variety and versatility of the crafts and also to produce quite different pieces. They have been loosely classified into toys, decorative pieces and personal items, and are identified as such with a motif above the main picture.

The projects in each chapter are arranged roughly in order of difficulty, allowing you to try your hand at simpler ones first if you wish. Always check the list of materials required for a project before you start. Alternative utensils can sometimes be substituted for those you may not already have. Read all the instructions through before undertaking the first step. If any of the terms used are unfamiliar to you, read the introduction to that chapter for clarification.

Most of the projects can be finished within a few hours. One or two, such as the découpage tray or the mosaic tile, require more time and some patience. All of them, however, will prove rewarding and inspire you to try out new ideas.

Converting Measurements

The measurements given in this book are in the imperial system and expressed as inches (") or feet ('). If you need to convert these, multiply each inch by 25.4 to get a metric measurement in millimetres. For example, 2 inches = 51 mm, which is equal to 5.1 cm. Below are the closest equivalents in the metric measurement system.

inches	mm	cm	inches	cm	inches	cm
$1/8$	3	0.3	$2 1/4$	5.7	8	20.3
$1/4$	6	0.6	$2 1/2$	6.4	9	22.9
$3/8$	10	1.0	$2 3/4$	7	10	25.4
$1/2$	13	1.3	3	7.6	11	27.9
$5/8$	16	1.6	$3 1/2$	8.9	12	30.5
$3/4$	20	2.0	4	10.2	13	33
$7/8$	22	2.2	$4 1/2$	11.4	14	35.6
1	25	2.5	5	12.7	15	38.1
$1 1/4$	32	3.2	$5 1/2$	14	16	40.6
$1 1/2$	38	3.8	6	15.2	17	43.2
$1 5/8$	40	4.0	$6 1/2$	16	18	45.7
$1 3/4$	45	4.5	7	17.8	19	48.3
2	50	5.0	$7 1/2$	18	20	50.8

Papermaking

Paper plays such a fundamental role in our lives that many people never stop to consider how it is made. Paper is a layer of intertwined fibers from a plant source which has been soaked and beaten to form a pulp. A two-section screen known as the mold and deckle is dipped into a mixture of pulp and water and the resulting sheet of fibers is drained and pressed.

These basic techniques have changed little over the nineteen centuries since the Chinese developed them. The main change has been the degree of mechanization in the process. In commercial mills, paper is formed on a moving belt which gives it a grain direction. It is finished, coated and cut so that sheets are uniform. One of the best qualities of handmade paper is its irregularity.

Any material containing cellulose fiber can be used for making paper at home, as long as it can be broken down. Waste paper, soaked overnight, can be pulped in a blender. Plant matter, such as celery, rhubarb and corn husks, must be boiled and beaten to break it down.

The most important piece of equipment is the mold and deckle. The mold is a frame which has a mesh stretched tight across it. The deckle is an unmeshed frame of the same size which traps the pulp on the mold. These can be bought in craft stores or you can make one from timber and nylon mesh.

You will need a plastic tub large enough for maneuvering the mold and deckle. Once formed, wet paper is "couched" by laying it on a damp cloth resting on a folded towel. Each sheet of paper is covered with another damp cloth. The cloth's texture will be transferred onto the paper: felt gives a smooth finish, quite unlike that created by linen. Two solid boards are useful for pressing the layers of paper.

Beyond these requirements are many optional extras. Writing paper should be "sized" by coating it with gelatine or another sealing solution. Color and textures can be added in a variety of ways. The paper pulp can also be used as a modeling material.

Your first efforts in papermaking may produce something quite unique and with only a bit of practice you will be forming beautiful sheets. The experience will certainly give you a better understanding and appreciation of paper in general.

A mold can be used without a deckle as in the first project, but only thin sheets can be formed in this way.

1 To recycle waste paper, tear into small scraps and soak in water overnight. Place a handful of scraps in a blender and fill it two-thirds with water. Blend for fifteen seconds. Half-fill a plastic tub with water and add six batches of blended pulp.

2 Stir the mixture. Hold the mold mesh-side up with the deckle tightly on top. Dip the mold and deckle vertically into the tub, level them under the surface and lift them straight up to catch a layer of pulp in the mesh. While water drains through the mesh, agitate the mold and deckle gently from side to side to even out the pulp.

3 Remove the deckle and tip the mold so that the paper lies on the couching mound (a damp cloth on a folded towel). Roll away the mold, ensuring that no pulp sticks to it. Cover the sheet with a damp cloth and repeat the process. Press the layers of paper and cloth between heavy boards overnight. Hang each cloth-and-sheet to dry. When dry, peel paper off the cloth.

Small petals, seeds and leaves can be added to the pulp before forming the sheet. Larger objects should be laid onto the wet sheet while still in the mold, which is then dipped a second time.

Color can be added by using colored waste paper, food dyes or natural materials such as brown onion skins.

Watermarks are made by attaching a thin wire shape to the mesh of the mold.

PROJECT 1

Pastel Doilies

YOU WILL NEED

paper scraps
food dyes
a blender
a large bowl
a small sewing hoop
muslin or netting
clean cloths
scissors
a towel
an iron

These dainty rounds of paper are easy to create using household equipment and are a good introduction to papermaking. They can be pressed flat or given a delicate raised edge.

1 ▸ Separate waste paper into different colors and tear into small squares. Soak in water overnight and blend to form batches of thick pulp. If extra color is needed, add a few drops of food coloring. Cut pieces of muslin or netting to fit your hoop. Fix in hoop so that the fabric is taut.

2 ▸ Pour a batch of pulp into a large bowl and stir so that the mixture is even. Dip the hoop vertically into the mixture and turn it so that it lies horizontally, with the mesh on the top. Lift the hoop straight out so that pulp is collected evenly on the mesh. Allow some water to drain off into the basin.

3 ▸ Lay the hoop, with the pulp facing down, on a damp cloth. Undo the fastening and carefully remove the inner hoop with the mesh.

4 ▸ Place another cloth on top so that the paper and muslin are sandwiched. Iron this sandwich dry, making sure no creases develop. Hold the paper disk and peel off the muslin. For a cupped effect, place a weight in the center and leave it to dry completely. For a flat doily, press the paper under several books.

PROJECT 2

Solitaire

This game for one player was invented in France during the eighteenth century. A lightweight but durable board can be made from paper pulp; all you need to add are the marbles!

1 Collect used envelopes which have a blue lining. Tear these and white waste paper into small scraps and soak them in water for a few hours. For an 8 " tin you will need 5 ounces of paper. Place a handful of scraps in a blender and fill two-thirds with water. Blend to form a thick pulp.

2 Pour the pulp into a large sieve and allow water to drain out for a minute. Tip the pulp into a cake pan with a removable base. Continue to blend and sieve until the pulp is 1 " or more deep in the pan.

The game: Start with a marble in every hole except for the center one. Jump one marble over an adjacent one, then remove the one which has been jumped over. Continue with the aim of ending with only one marble left, in the center hole.

3 With a kitchen sponge, press down onto the pulp and remove excess water. Stop when the pulp becomes resistant to a finger's pressure.

4 Position 33 marbles in a grid of 7 x 7 rows to form a cross. Press them down halfway into the pulp and leave in the pan for 24 hours. Remove the board from the cake pan and allow it to dry on a wire rack; this may take several days. Apply a layer of acrylic varnish and decorate with a strip of card or a ribbon.

PROJECT 3

Notebooks

Handmade paper is lovely to look at and to write on, although it must be coated with size before it can be written on with a calligraphy or fountain pen.

YOU WILL NEED
paper materials
starch
gelatin
a mold & deckle
a plastic tub
a blender
cloths & a towel
a brush
a needle
gold thread

1 ◀ Prepare a paper pulp and add petals and leaves. Add a tablespoon of starch, dissolved in hot water. Prepare a couching mound. Pour the pulp into a large plastic tub and stir it. Dip the mold and deckle into the pulp and raise it to form a sheet. For more information on these techniques, see pages 16-17.

2 ◀ Remove the deckle and tip the mold so that the paper lies on the couching mound. Cover with a damp cloth and repeat the process. Your first sheet will probably be the thickest. Press the pile of sheets between heavy boards overnight and then hang to dry. For more information, see page 17.

3 ▶ When the paper is quite dry, size it with gelatin. Dissolve a teaspoon of gelatin in 5 cups of hot water and brush this solution onto the paper with a wide soft brush. Leave it to dry, then turn the paper and coat the other side.

4 ◀ Fold each sheet of paper in half. Using the thickest sheet as a cover, insert three or four sheets to form a booklet. Pierce the inside center with a needle and strong thread. Return the needle 1" higher up the fold. Make a third stitch 1" below the first hole and bring the needle back through the center. Tie the thread ends.

Papier-mâché

Although the name is French in origin, the art of mashed paper was developed by the Chinese, shortly after they had invented paper itself. That it was used to make warriors' helmets testifies to the strength of papier-mâché. That it was also used for children's toys says something of its creative potential.

In this craft, strips of torn paper are pasted together to form lightweight but substantial objects. It is a relatively slow but extremely inexpensive method of sculpting and it offers almost unlimited possibilities in the shapes and decorative effects you can achieve.

There are various options for forming pieces. Paper can be pasted onto an existing object, encasing cardboard shapes or covering a surface of a plate and using it as a mold. Hollow receptacles can be made by pasting paper over molded clay or a balloon. Perhaps the best example of this type are the pinatas of Mexico, papier-mâché shapes filled with sweets and burst in festival games. Molds can also be used to create objects with detail such as masks or toy animals. Larger scale projects can be built up over an armature, a structure made of wire, wood, cardboard, bottles or whatever suits the purpose. Such extra materials are also useful to add strength to delicate or slender sections of a piece.

For the base layers, it is most economical to use strips of newspaper. By using a different colored newspaper every second layer you will be sure to cover the object evenly. As a finish, you can use strips of colored tissue paper for the final layer or the object can be sealed and brightly painted.

Papier-mâché offers great scope for creativity whether you are making practical objects or purely decorative ones. Eighteenth century Europeans used it to make pieces of furniture, but smaller projects could include chunky jewelry, figurines and elaborate frames. It is especially useful for making puppet heads which need to be light and hollow.

Wallpaper paste is ideal for pasting the paper together. If it isn't available, mix up a paste from flour and water.

1 Half-fill a bowl with water. Sprinkle on wallpaper paste and stir well with a fork. Leave the paste for ten minutes, stirring it occasionally. Prepare the mold by shaping modeling clay, cutting card shapes or coating dishes with petroleum jelly.

2 Tear plenty of newspaper strips along the grain. The size of the strips will depend on the size and type of project. If working on a very small item, tear these strips into squares. Do not cut the paper: the feathered edge of torn paper results in a smoother finish.

3 Dip strips into the paste and remove excess with your fingers. Apply the pieces to the mold, overlapping them and smoothing each one down. Only a few layers are needed to cover a card shape; up to eight are necessary on larger projects. Allow the paper to dry. Coat with gesso or acrylic house paint before decorating it.

These beads have been formed around modeling clay. They were cut open, the clay removed and another layer pasted over the cut.

A single layer of tissue paper creates a rich hue when pasted over the coat of gesso.

PROJECT 4

Striped Bowl

YOU WILL NEED
paper in two colors
newspaper
petroleum jelly
a bowl
paste
a brush
scissors
matte varnish

Papier-mâché objects don't have to be painted in bright colors. Instead, you can use pastel papers to finish your piece, in this case a pretty bowl.

1 Tear newspaper into strips 1 " wide. Mix up a paste (see page 25). Coat the inside of a bowl with petroleum jelly. Dip newspaper strips into the paste and remove excess paste with your fingers. Work from the center out, applying overlapping strips around the inside of the bowl. Allow strips to overlap the rim by 1 ".

2 Apply eight layers of newspaper strips and leave 24 hours to dry. Remove from the mold and allow base to dry. Tear a 2 x 8 " piece of newspaper, coat it with paste and form a long thin roll. Position it on the base of the bowl and hold it in place with pasted strips. Allow to dry.

3 Tear narrow strips of paper in two colors. Dip them in paste and apply them, alternating the colors, around the inside and outside of the bowl. Finish with a tapered piece. Allow to dry. Trim the rim of the bowl with scissors, leaving a ½ " lip.

4 Tear 1 " squares in one color and paste them over the rim to neaten the cut edge and form a band of color. Leave to dry. Apply several coats of matte varnish, allowing each coat to dry before applying the next.

PROJECT 5

Maracas

Traditionally, these percussion instruments were made from hollowed gourds and filled with pebbles or seeds. Papier-mâché maracas can make just as much noise!

1 ◄ Mold modeling clay to form two heads with protruding necks. Mix up a paste (see page 25). Tear newspaper into ½ " squares and coat them in paste. Apply six layers of overlapping squares onto the heads. Allow to dry, then cut each head in half and remove the modeling clay.

2 ► Roll a 6 " square piece of card tightly and secure it with paste. Roll this in a 5 " square piece of newspaper coated with paste. Repeat with a 4 " square of newspaper to form a handle with a slight bulge in the middle. Repeat the whole process to form a second handle.

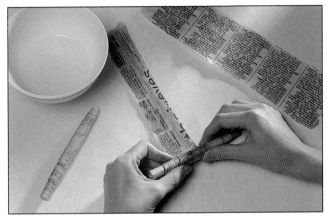

3 ► Place a tablespoon of rice grains in one half of a head and lay the handle in the neck section. Apply glue around the rim and neck and place the other head piece on top. Hold in place with masking tape until glue is dry. Paste newspaper strips over the joins.

4 ► Seal maracas with a coat of white gesso. Use masking tape to cover some sections while you paint several coats of the first color. When dry, reposition the masking tape and paint the other sections in the second color. Add detail with a gold pen, then varnish.

PROJECT 6

Candle Holder

This papier-mâché project is constructed with a cardboard handle and collar. A few strokes with a gold pen add the stars which will light you to bed.

YOU WILL NEED
newspaper
card
petroleum jelly
a plate
paste & glue
scissors
a brush
blue gesso
gold pen
gloss varnish

1 ▶ Coat the base of a plate with petroleum jelly. Mix up a paste (see page 25). Tear newspaper into strips 1" wide, dip them in paste and remove excess with your fingers. Apply eight layers of overlapping strips onto the plate base. Allow to dry for 24 hours, then remove the disk from the mold.

2 ▶ Trim around the rim neatly with scissors. Cut a strip of card and glue it to form a collar which fits your candle base. Glue the collar to the center of the disk and secure it with strips of pasted newspaper. Bind the rim of the base with a layer of pasted strips.

3 ◀ Cut a strip of card to form a handle and glue one edge on top of the rim and the other on the underneath. Secure the handle with pasted strips. Allow the candle holder to dry thoroughly.

4 ▶ Paint the candle holder with blue gesso (or prime with white gesso and then paint blue) and allow it to dry. With a gold pen, draw stars and gild the rim and handle edges. Apply a coat of gloss acrylic varnish.

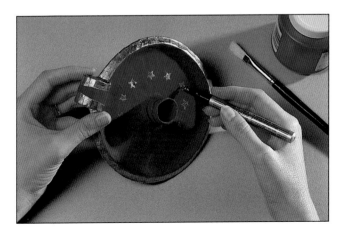

Weaving

Few craft techniques are as ancient and widespread as that of weaving. The regular interlacing of threads to form a cloth is a traditional skill in most cultures and each ethnic group has explored its decorative potential through different designs, textures and colorings.

Paper, like thread, can be woven to create a larger piece of material, to increase its strength or simply to add decorative interest. The use of paper is an excellent and inexpensive way to learn the basics of weaving and, although you will not be able to achieve the complexity of a loom-woven fabric, you can still create imaginative and interesting pieces. Paper or flexible card can be woven to form sturdy boxes, colorful wall hangings, unique jewelry, or any number of attractive and useful things.

When weaving in a block, vertical strips are known as warp strips; horizontal strips make up the weft. Using a craft knife and metal ruler, cut the warp strips along the grain to give added support, while the weft strips should be cut across the grain for flexibility. Alternatively, you could tear strips of paper for a softer effect. Combine strips of different colors and try cutting them in varying widths and at irregular angles. Changing the color series of the warp and weft or the sequence of threading over-and-under, will give quite different effects, as shown on the top of the next page. Experiment by weaving strips of paper with other materials such as ribbon, twigs or twine.

There are many variations on the warp-and-weft method of weaving. Paper strips can be woven through slots in a contrasting sheet of paper or card to create a dramatic effect. Braiding or plaiting allows you to quickly weave strips into a narrow band or tape. The projects in this chapter explore each of these three basic techniques as a starting point in paper weaving.

Weave a few strips through a tag to add a touch of style.

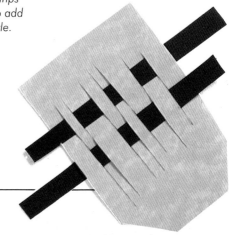

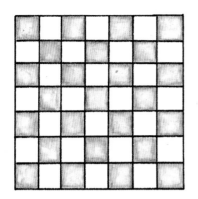

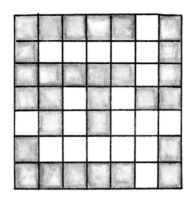

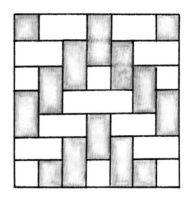

Warp and weft variations
Different patterns can be made by varying the color of the warp and weft strips or by jumping over more than one strip at a time. A plain or "tabby" weave uses one color for warp and another for weft and weaves them in a regular "over-and-under-one" pattern.

A random design made by varying the colors used for warp and weft strips.

A zigzag pattern created by jumping over two warp strips.

Slit-and-slot designs
These simple motifs are woven by slitting paper and slotting a contrasting color through. They would make a good alternative crest for the stationery project on page 34.
  For the top motif, draw a circle intersected by a vertical line. Cut along the lines, breaking the circle on both sides of the vertical line. Weave two black strips through to form quadrants.

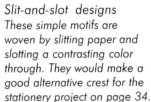

Danish hearts
This traditional design is created by weaving two halves of a heart which have been folded and slotted. The steps below show how to create the simpler heart that appears at the top of page 34.

PROJECT 7

Personal Letters

YOU WILL NEED
light-colored paper
contrasting paper
a pencil
a ruler
glue
an eraser
a knife & mat

With a simple slot-and-strip weave you can represent most letters of the alphabet. Put two at the crest of attractive writing paper and you have personalized stationery.

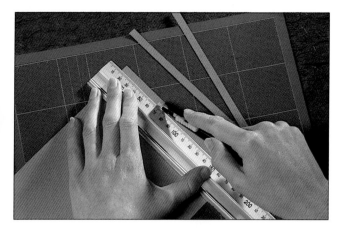

1 Cut dark-colored paper into strips ³/₈ " wide. Cut light-colored paper into pieces 9 x 6½ ", or use writing paper which has been cut to size.

2 Rule a pencil line ½ " from the top of the writing paper. Rule a parallel line ½ " below, another ¼ " below that and a fourth line ½ " below that. Sketch the letter shapes and cut the appropriate slits with a sharp knife. Erase all pencil lines.

3 Starting from the back, weave a dark strip through the top set of slits and a second through the bottom slits. Glue the ends of the strips on the back of the writing paper.

4 Cut envelopes to fit your folded writing sheets using an old envelope as a basic pattern. Glue down the side flaps and weave letters on the top flap.

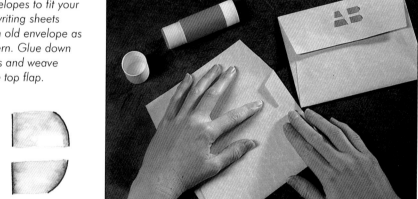

PROJECT 8

Checkers Set

YOU WILL NEED
heavy black card
thin colored card
a pencil
a ruler
a knife & mat
an eraser
a compass
scissors
glue

The game of checkers is played on the same board as chess and both games date back more than a thousand years. The woven playing pieces in this set are "crowned" on one side.

1 ◀ Cut eight strips of pale card measuring 12 x 1½ ". Cut dark card into a 12 " square. Rule a ³/₈ " margin along the right and left sides. Rule a ³/₈ " margin along the top and mark at 1½ " intervals. Make corresponding marks along the base and cut between the pairs of marks.

3 ▼ Using the dark card as the warp or vertical bars, weave a pale strip under and over, under and over. Ease it up towards the margin. Weave the next one over and under and so on, to create a plain weave. Make sure the horizontal strips are evenly spaced in the warp.

2 ▲ Cut two 13 " squares of heavy black card. In the middle of one, cut a 12 " square, creating a 1 " frame. Sandwich the woven card between the base and the frame and glue to secure. Press under a stack of books until glue is dry.

4 ▶ Cut disks with a 1¼ " diameter: 24 on thin black card, 12 pale and 12 dark. Cut eight slits around the colored disks, cutting halfway in. Cut a slit in the black disks and then cut out a circle with a ⁵/₈ " diameter. Weave a black collar around each colored disk. Glue on the black dot to signify the crowned side.

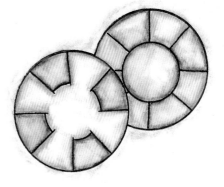

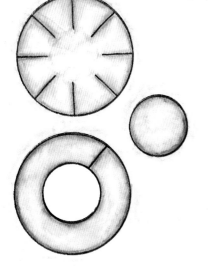

PROJECT 9

Napkin Rings

YOU WILL NEED
black card
card in two colors
a knife & mat
glue
a ruler
double-sided tape

Braided paper forms quite a sturdy band and these napkin rings will serve well for many special occasions. Choose colors to complement the tableware or a set of napkins.

1. For each ring, you will need a 7 x 1¼ " piece of black card and three 10 x ½ " strips in different colors. Cut these pieces along the grain of the card. Glue the ends of the black rectangle together to form a collar.

2. Tape one end of the three strips to a piece of scrap card. Fold the right strip over the center strip, left over right, center over left, and so on, to form a braid. The diagram on the right provides a useful reference.

3. When the strips are fully braided, attach a length of double-sided tape along the back and wrap the braid around a black collar.

4. Weave the ends of the strips in and secure with glue or double-sided tape. Make a box base from black card and attach a braided handle, making sure rings can be easily removed.

Découpage

Découpage, from the French verb *découper* - "to cut", has a fascinating history. Lacquered pieces of furniture, imported from the Orient, were highly valued in seventeenth century Europe. To meet the demand at a lower price, Venetian craftsmen developed a process of pasting paper prints and covering them with the recently invented varnish. The mass-produced prints were painstakingly hand-painted and cut out by apprentices. Once submerged under many layers of varnish, these images appeared to be painted onto the wood itself.

The French court of the eighteenth century had a taste for the ornate and took up découpage as a pastime in the period before the revolution.

Victorians adopted and adapted the craft, applying their own taste for high sentiment. It became a craze and new color printing methods supplied the devotees with a huge range of purpose-printed cherubs and flower baskets.

There has been a recent resurgence in the craft's popularity, with enough latitude to accommodate everyone's tastes. Serious découpers insist on countless layers of varnish. This adds depth to the finish, but if it detracts from your enjoyment then it is not necessary. The projects in this chapter are fairly free interpretations of découpage techniques: they all involve careful cutting, pasting and covering.

The most important aspect of découpage is the cutting and arrangement of the images. A small pair of sharp scissors with curved blades and a good eye are essential. Popular objects for decorating are boxes, trays and screens, but any object with a flat or gently rounded surface can be worked on.

Images can be cut from magazines, books, old greeting cards or giftwrap.

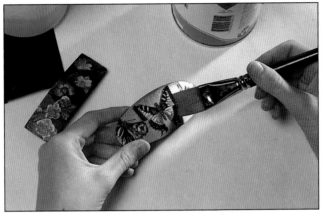

1 ◄ If necessary, paint the object to be découpaged and then seal it with acrylic varnish. Seal your paper images and cut them out using scissors with curved blades. Glue the images onto the object, making sure no air is trapped. When dry, wipe off any excess glue and pencil over any white edges.

2 ► Seal the piece. Apply multiple coats of polyurethane varnish, brushing each coat in a different direction. Keep the surface free of dust. Once the images are well covered, sand lightly with very fine wet-&-dry paper. Apply a final coat of varnish.

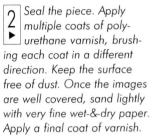

Painting photocopied drawings with watercolors imitates the original style of découpage.

Wet-&-dry paper, fine steel wool and an anti-dust cloth all help achieve a perfect finish.

PROJECT 10

Portfolio

You don't need to be a musician to appreciate this stylish folder for holding notes and documents. Photocopies of music will do just as well as the real thing.

YOU WILL NEED

sheet music
white card
gold card
adhesive covering
scissors
a knife & mat
glue
a pencil & ruler
string
paper fasteners

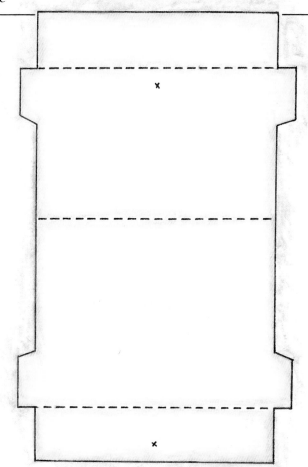

1 ▲ *Cut a piece of white card 15 x 24 ". Enlarge the pattern to 500%, mark it on the card and cut out the portfolio. Glue whole sheets of music to cover the card. Use a small pair of scissors to cut out extra bars of music and glue these over any gaps.*

2 ▼ *Score along dotted lines on the outside of the portfolio with a sharp knife. Cover with clear plastic adhesive, leaving the tabs uncovered. Fold and flatten with weights.*

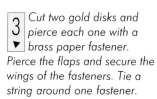

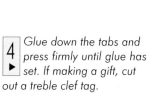

3 ▼ *Cut two gold disks and pierce each one with a brass paper fastener. Pierce the flaps and secure the wings of the fasteners. Tie a string around one fastener.*

4 ▶ *Glue down the tabs and press firmly until glue has set. If making a gift, cut out a treble clef tag.*

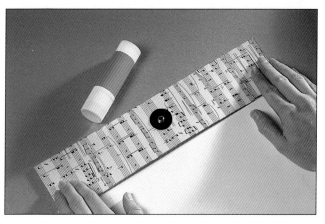

PROJECT 11

Puzzle Blocks

Puzzle blocks are a delightful traditional game to be cherished by every child. Choose images with plenty of detail and of a similar style; storybook pictures are ideal.

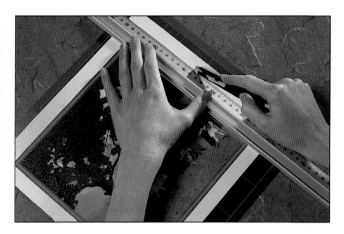

1 Select six pictures of a similar size. Take the smallest picture and determine how many 1½" square pieces can be cut from it; this will be the required number of blocks. Crop all the pictures to this multiple of 1½".

2 Rule up a 1½" grid on a sheet of card and map out a series of crosses; one cross per required block. Cut out these crosses and score along the fold lines to form small boxes.

3 Tape the sides of each box with tape. Using a sharp knife and cutting mat, cut the first picture into 1½" squares. Keep the squares in sequence.

4 Paste each of the squares onto a block. Arrange the blocks to form the picture and then turn them over in rows. Cut and paste the next picture, turn the blocks in rows, and so on until they are fully covered. When the glue is dry, coat blocks with acrylic varnish. Make a box for them and, if you have a spare picture, glue it on the lid.

Suggestion: For a longer lasting toy, cut square blocks from wood offcuts.

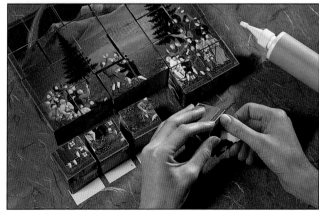

PROJECT 12

Découpage Tray

Turn a tray into a work of art using basic découpage techniques. The images used in this example are from giftwrap created by the artist Jane Ray.

YOU WILL NEED
a wooden tray
paper prints
scissors
a brush
a sponge
acrylic paint
glue
sealer
varnish
wet-&-dry paper

1 ▶ Prepare the surface of the tray. If it is old wood, strip off any paint and sand smooth. The tray shown has been painted with gesso, followed by a coat of blue acrylic paint which was dabbed with a sea sponge for a mottled effect. Apply a coat of sealer.

2 ◀ Select suitable images for the base and sides of the tray. Before cutting them out, apply a coat of sealer to both sides of the printed image. When dry, cut out images carefully with a small pair of scissors.

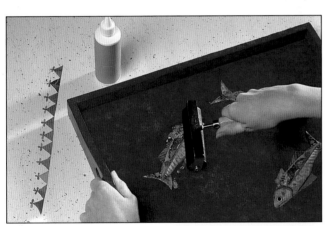

3 ◀ Plan the arrangement of images on the tray, before gluing them down one at a time. Smear glue onto the tray with your fingertips and lay the cut image down. Smooth it out, checking for air bubbles. Paste down all the images in this way. When glue has set, wipe excess away with a damp sponge. Pencil over any white edges.

4 ◀ Seal the whole tray. When dry, varnish it, brushing in one direction only. Allow to dry in a dust-free environment. Apply 20 or so coats of varnish, changing the direction of your brush-strokes with each coat. With very fine wet-&-dry paper, sand in one direction and then another. Wipe clean and apply a final coat of varnish.

Papercuts

Folk cultures all around the world have traditions of papercutting. In China, it was given the name *chien-chih*. In Germany and Switzerland, it is known as *scherenschnitte*. To the Dutch, it is *knippen*. The ancient Mexican peoples, the Japanese, the Jews: all developed their own style of cutting paper in a decorative manner.

Some themes are cross-cultural: religious scenes and texts, images from nature and symbols of love and good fortune often featured in cutwork. In some countries, documents and certificates were elaborately decorated with papercuts. The German migrants who settled in America during the late seventeenth century brought a tradition of cutting and coloring elaborate valentines making declarations of love and even proposals of marriage. The cutting of shadow portraits or silhouettes was extremely popular in France and England in the late eighteenth century, before the invention of the camera.

Methods of cutting paper varied from country to country. In China, up to fifty sheets of very fine paper are cut using a pattern. These are sometimes dyed to form a multi-colored design. Scherenschnitte pieces are usually cut on paper which has been folded once, creating a symmetrical image in a single color.

Some people like to cut designs with a knife while others prefer scissors: a combination of the two can be ideal. If you are using a knife, a cutting mat is essential.

Papercutting has many applications. Use it to decorate frames or greeting cards or to make doilies. A strip of paper folded and cut with a repeat pattern produces beautiful shelf edging or paper ribbon. Papercuts can also serve as templates in embroidery and quilting.

Silhouettes
Cast a shadow and trace it on white paper. Scale this down, transfer it onto black paper and cut the image out.

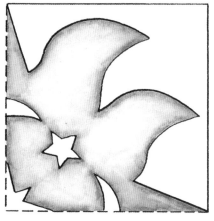

Tree of life
Many traditional papercutters favour this subject. Use this example as a pattern. It is a mirror image, so your tracing can be flipped to complete the design.

Snowflakes
By folding and cutting a square piece of paper, you can create endless pretty variations. The top two designs are for four-part folds, that is, a square which has been folded in half and then in half again. The third design is for an eight-part fold, made by folding the above an extra time. The finished design appears at the top of page 48.

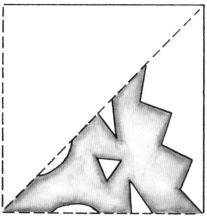

Paper dolls
This design is worked on the same principles as a chain of paper dolls. Cut a long strip of paper, fold it in a concertina and cut the pattern.

PROJECT 13

Shadow Puppets

Flat cutout figures can take on a life of their own when held against a translucent screen. This courting couple are based on traditional Polish papercut figures.

YOU WILL NEED
black card
tracing paper
a ballpoint pen
a knife & mat
colored cellophane
tape.
glue
clothes-hanger wire
pliers
strong tape

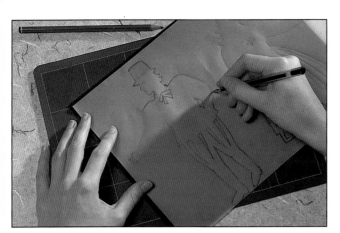

1 *Enlarge the patterns by 200% and transfer them onto black card, using tracing paper and a ballpoint pen. Using a sharp craft knife or scalpel, remove the cutout sections first and then cut the whole figure from the card. If you want to move the puppets in both directions, cut out two versions of each character.*

2 *Cut pieces of colored cellophane slightly larger than the cutout sections and tape them on the back of each figure.*

Suggestion: Make a screen from tissue paper or thin fabric pulled taut. Natural daylight or a desk lamp provides suitable back lighting.

3 *Bend one end of a 12" length of clothes-hanger or stiff wire to form a flat loop. Cut a strip of card and thread it through the loop. Mold the card around the wire then glue the flaps to the back of the puppet. Bind the end of the wire with strong tape to form a handle.*

PROJECT 14

Oriental Jewelry

A hint of gold and black lacquer summon up the riches of the Orient in this brooch and earring set. Take care not to use too much glue as this can spoil the effect.

YOU WILL NEED
black card
gold card
tracing paper
a pencil
a knife & mat
glue
a brush
acrylic varnish
wire
brooch & earring wires

1 ▶ *Transfer the patterns onto black card using tracing paper and a pencil. With a sharp knife, remove the cutout sections first and then cut the whole shape from the card. You will need a single circular shape and four diamonds. Cut a backing disk, this time in solid black.*

2 ◀ *Cut solid shapes in gold card, slightly smaller than the black shapes. Apply a coat of acrylic varnish to each of the black cutouts and to the backing disk.*

3 ▲ *Apply a tiny amount of glue to the back of the circle cutout and attach it to the gold disk. Glue this combination onto the backing disk. Finally, attach the brooch pin with glue.*

4 ▶ *Apply a tiny amount of glue to the back of each black diamond and back with a gold piece. Thread a length of wire through the loop of the earring wire and twist to secure, then glue it onto the back of a diamond. Glue the two halves of each earring together.*

PROJECT 15

Potpourri Box

YOU WILL NEED
cream card
heavy white card
a pencil
tracing paper
a compass
scissors
glue
a knife & mat

*Sweet-smelling potpourri deserves a pretty container.
The papercut lid on this shallow box allows the scent to
escape and gives a glimpse of colorful petals inside.*

1 With a compass and a pencil, draw a circle with a 2¾" radius on cream card. Cut this out and score a line lightly down the center of the disk. Gently fold in half. Transfer the pattern in pencil. Cut out the pattern with a sharp knife.

2 Erase any pencil marks left on the lid. Make a fillet for the lid by cutting a circular band approximately ¼" wide in heavy white card. The fillet should be slightly smaller than the decorative lid. Glue the fillet to the underside of the lid.

3 Cut a strip of cream card measuring 2" wide and 17½" long. Score a line along the length, ½" in from the edge. Cut triangular tabs at ½" intervals. Glue the end of the strip together with an overlap of 1", to form a large cylinder.

4 Cut two cream disks, one with a radius of 2⅝" and the other ⅛" smaller. Ease the smaller disk into the cylinder and glue down the tabs of the strip to secure the base. Glue the larger disk on the outside base to conceal the tabs. Fill the box with potpourri.

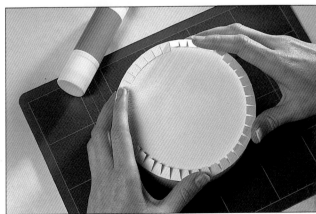

Dimensionals

Many of the papercrafts enjoyed today have been revived from the Victorian era, when women's journals turned certain crafts into fashionable pastimes. Among these was the creation of three-dimensional scenes, known as *vue d'optique* or shadow boxes. Prints and drawings were carefully cut out, arranged in a tableau, mounted with cork backings to give a sense of depth and then encased in a glass-fronted box. Modern materials have changed the craft somewhat, but it is still alive and flourishing under such names as dimensional découpage or paper tole.

Dimensionals, as we will call them, can be created by layering découpage cutouts and backing them with silicone or thick double-sided tape. The most popular style, however, are made with a set of identical images: three or four for simple designs and up to eight for complex ones. An ideal source is a sheet of giftwrap with a repeat design. Greeting cards,

books and commercially available kits are other sources. So that you can reproduce the projects in this chapter, we have used kits: details are on page 160. Wherever the images come from, they must be sharply defined and contain elements which suggest perspective.

Only a few pieces of equipment are essential: a sharp craft knife or scalpel, a cutting mat, angled scissors and some silicone sealer. A soft pencil is useful for coloring edges and a cocktail stick can be used to maneuver small pieces. Pieces can be shaped with the bowl of a teaspoon or with a purpose-bought shaping tool and mat. Acrylic varnish is needed for sealing prints and can be used to add highlights or a protective finish.

Dimensionals can be framed, or can be used as a frame themselves. Recessed box lids, greeting cards and Christmas decorations are all interesting ways to display dimensionals.

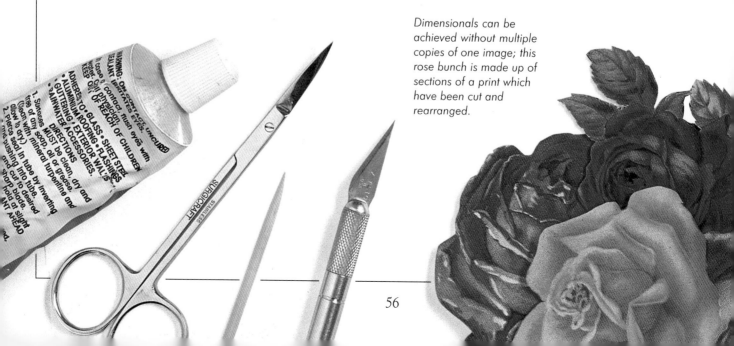

Dimensionals can be achieved without multiple copies of one image; this rose bunch is made up of sections of a print which have been cut and rearranged.

© PTC 1994

© PTC 1994

1 ▲ *Plan your design carefully to assess which pieces should be raised. Seal the back of the prints with acrylic varnish. Carefully cut the pieces, cutting multiples of the foreground pieces and overcutting where necessary. With a soft lead pencil, color any cut edges where the white paper is visible.*

Line-drawings can be photocopied, colored with pencil or paint, sealed, and used as a set of prints.

2 ▲ *Shape pieces which would naturally be rounded or curved. Apply a spot of silicone to the back of pieces and attach them to a base print. Apply enough silicone to raise the image by $\frac{1}{8}$" but not so much that it can be seen. Continue to build up the layers. Highlight sections (or coat the whole piece) with high gloss acrylic varnish.*

Overcut adjacent sections where the cut edges would otherwise be visible.

PROJECT 16

Floral Picture

Images of flowers are ideal for creating dimension. Whether it be a small card or a framed picture, layered petals and leaves add a pleasing sense of depth.

YOU WILL NEED
a set of prints
white card
a knife & mat
acrylic varnish
a brush
silicone
a shaping tool
framing materials

1 ▶ *Choose a suitable print: you will need multiple copies of it. Seal the back of the prints with acrylic varnish before cutting. Plan which sections will be layered and raised. Leave one print uncut as the base image. With a sharp knife, cut one whole image and multiples of each of the sections to be raised.*

2 ◀ *Paste the base image onto white card. Make sure there are no creases. Apply silicone where it will not be visible and lay down the complete cutout, positioning it carefully over the base image and pressing gently to ensure the paper adheres to the silicone.*

3 ◀ *Shape pieces such as petals by gently molding them with a rounded tool. Apply a small amount of silicone to the back of each piece and stick in place. Build up the layers of sections which would protrude: foreground flowers and leaves, sepals, or whatever is appropriate.*

4 ▶ *Apply several coats of high gloss acrylic varnish to those areas which you wish to highlight. Frame the finished picture with foam spacers between the mounts so the layered image does not project beyond the frame.*

Suggestion: The same principles can be used to make a smaller project such as this greeting card, presented in a mount with three panels.

PROJECT 17

Photo Frame

© PTC 1994

YOU WILL NEED
a set of prints
a knife & mat
acrylic varnish
a brush
silicone
glue
thick card
tracing paper
a ruler
a pencil & marking pen

Everyone has a favorite photograph which deserves a special frame. You will need multiple copies of a border design or you could draw, photocopy and color your own.

1 ▶ Trace the pattern for the stand onto thick card then cut and score. Cut a rectangle from the card and glue the photograph in the center. Color the edges of the mount with a thick marking pen so they will be less obtrusive. Glue the stand onto the back so that the wider end is at the base.

© PTC 1994

2 ▲ Choose a suitable print: you will need multiple copies. Seal the back of the prints with acrylic varnish. Plan which pieces should be raised. With a sharp knife, cut one complete image (the base image) and multiples of each of the sections to be raised.

3 ▶ Apply a small amount of silicone onto the back of each piece and position it carefully over the base image. Shape pieces, such as the curved balloon or the curling ribbon, before sticking them in place.

© PTC 1994

4 ▶ Apply several coats of high gloss acrylic varnish to those areas which you wish to highlight. Glue the border onto the card backing using silicone.

© PTC 1994

61

PROJECT 18

Toy Theater

This miniature theater is ideal for small hands and can be filled with a range of favorite characters. The stage may be made to measure or cut from an empty tissue box.

YOU WILL NEED
a set of prints
a knife & mat
acrylic varnish
a brush
silicone
thick white card
gold spray paint
a ruler
a compass
skewers or toothpicks

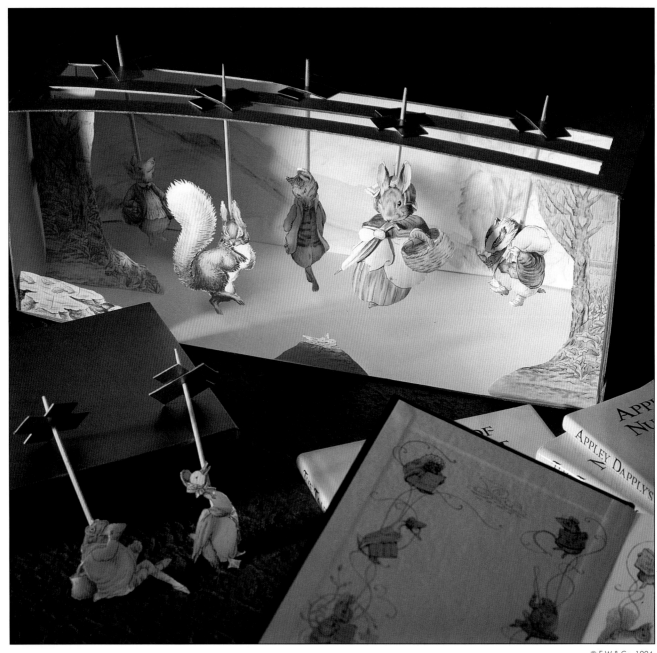

1 ◄ Cut a 12 x 19 " piece of card to form a box 11 " long, 4 " wide and 4 " deep. Cut two $^3/_8$ " wide slots as shown. Spray one side of all the pieces gold. Glue the tabs to form the box. Keep the gold strips for use later.

2 ▲ Cut a 4 x 11 " piece of paper and paint a simple backdrop. Paste this to the inside back of the box. Cut background detail from prints (or paint some) and glue extra strips of paper on as tabs. Glue these to the sides of the box, keeping clear of the character slots.

© F W & Co. 1994

3 ► Seal the back of each print with acrylic gloss varnish and allow to dry before cutting out. Cut a base figure, then add layers of detail with a dab of silicone between each of the layers.

4 ► Attach each character to a toothpick with silicone. Cut the gold strips into 1 " lengths and glue in pairs to form crossbars. Pierce each crossbar with the point of a compass and push the top of a toothpick through the hole.

© F W & Co. 1994

Paper Mechanics

We generally think of paper as a static material, but opening a children's pop-up book makes us revise that opinion. In such a work, paper can be seen to swivel, spin, twist and spring. Peep into the inner workings of those pages and you have some insight into paper mechanics. This chapter is concerned with making paper move.

Despite the name, paper mechanics is not a new craft. Many traditional origami designs, such as the flapping crane or the fortune teller, are fine examples of such engineering.

Paper darts and gliders are some other old favorites. Paper can also be folded or cut in such a way that it harnesses the wind (or even just a breeze). Two of the projects in this chapter demonstrate how this can be done very simply.

Pop-ups can be constructed by various methods. Incised pop-ups are made by folding a sheet of paper in half, slitting it and creasing new folds. The incised pop-up opens to 90 degrees; once you open them 180 degrees the incised section returns to a flat position. Multi-piece pop-ups are designed to open completely and are formed by attaching various pieces to a backing card. The posy in Project 21 is an example of this type.

There are also many ways of creating movable joints in paper using hinges, axles and paper fasteners. When designing projects, it is wise to make a rough in scrap paper first. This allows you to check angles, folds and actions to ensure that the concept can be realized and the model will work smoothly.

Paper mechanics requires a logical approach but creativity plays a major role. Start with greeting cards or decorations and go on to explore such possibilities as toys and personalized pop-up books.

An axle made from two disks of paper allows a turning movement, while the "Chinese stairs" can be used as a spring.

This segmented snake slithers on joints fixed with paper fasteners.

▲ By cutting a design with hinges, you can twist sections of card out to create a three-dimensional image. This principle can also be applied to letters of the alphabet and numbers.

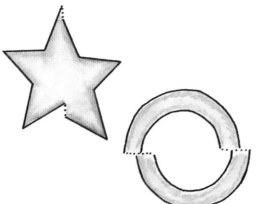

▲ Pop-ups intrigue us with their sudden change from two-dimensional pieces of paper to three-dimensional images. These are both multi-piece pop-ups, although the one on the left could have been made as an incised model. The star is basically a paper chain glued at the ends to a backing card.

Jumping jack

Examples of this type of toy have been enjoyed by children in countries around the world.

To make a jumping jack, cut out separate legs, arms and a body and decorate them. Pierce a hole at the top of each limb. Lay the body face down and arrange the pieces so that the limbs overlap with the body. Pierce a hole through both layers in the shoulders and tops of the legs. Use paper fasteners or knotted threads to attach the limbs to the body so that they can move freely.

With the limbs at a resting position, tie a string linking the two arms and another linking the two legs. Tie another string from the top link to the bottom link and allow it to hang below the jumping jack. Pulling this string should cause the legs and arms to swing upwards.

PROJECT 19

Twisting Prisms

YOU WILL NEED
foil-covered card
tracing paper
a pencil
a ruler
a knife & mat
gold thread
a needle
scissors

These eye-catching decorations are made using the cut-and-twist method. When hung from the bough of a tree they will spin and sparkle in the breeze.

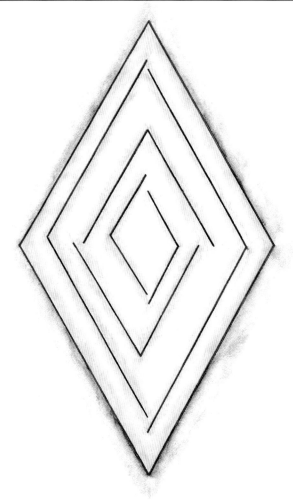

1 ▲ Transfer the pattern onto foil-covered card. Mark a vertical and horizontal center guideline. With a ruler and sharp knife, cut the pattern lines accurately.

2 ◄ Hold the rim and twist the rest of the prism so that it lies at an angle of 90 degrees to the rim. Twist the next frame so it lies horizontally. Twist the solid section in the center so that it lies on the same plane as the rim.

3 ► Secure the horizontal plane by twisting it through the rim and wedging it. Thread a needle with gold thread and pierce the top of the prism. Tie the thread in a loop.

PROJECT 20

Windmills

YOU WILL NEED

colored paper
dowel
a wooden hoop
glue & tape
curling ribbon
wire
a knife & mat
a large needle
map pins
a ballpoint pen

Here is a whole fleet of sails to spin in the breeze. A simpler version could be made with a single windmill on a skewer, using paper in a child's favorite color.

1 Cut a 16 " length of dowel. Wrap curling ribbon tightly around it and secure with tape. Do the same with the hoop. Glue the hoop to the dowel in two places and secure with wire or tape.

2 Glue sheets of paper in pairs so that they are a different color front and back. Cut the laminated paper into 3 " squares.

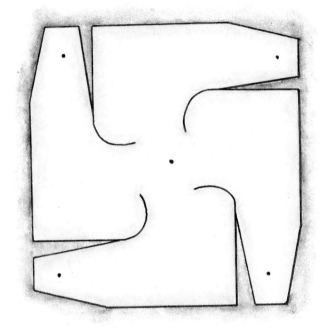

3 Cut the squares according to the pattern and make a hole at each corner with a large needle. Remove the ink tube from the ballpoint pen and cut ¼ " lengths off the empty end.

4 Bend each corner to the center and thread the flaps onto a map pin. Pierce the center and thread a piece of tubing onto the pin. Push the pin point securely into the hoop. Gently push the sails forward so the windmill spins freely when you blow. Attach each windmill in this way. Supervise very young children using the toy.

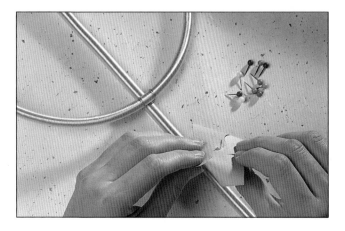

PROJECT 21

Pop-up Posy

Few things are nicer than receiving flowers from a friend. This charming bouquet has an added attraction: it can be sent through the post.

YOU WILL NEED
card in several colors
black card
glue
a pencil
tracing paper
a ruler
a knife & mat
a marking pen
scissors
ribbon

1 Enlarge all the patterns by 200%. Fold a piece of green card in two and transfer the foliage pattern so that the dashed line is aligned with the fold. Transfer the other patterns onto card of appropriate colors and cut all pieces out with a sharp knife. Glue the flowers onto the greenery.

2 Cut a 14 x 7" piece of card for the base. Score a line across the center and fold it in half to form a square. Score flaps in the greenery and glue them onto the base. Construct the pot around the greenery, testing that the card will open smoothly before gluing the pot flaps.

3 Color the flaps with a marker pen so that they are less obtrusive. Cut a slot at either edge of the base and tie a narrow ribbon through each slot.

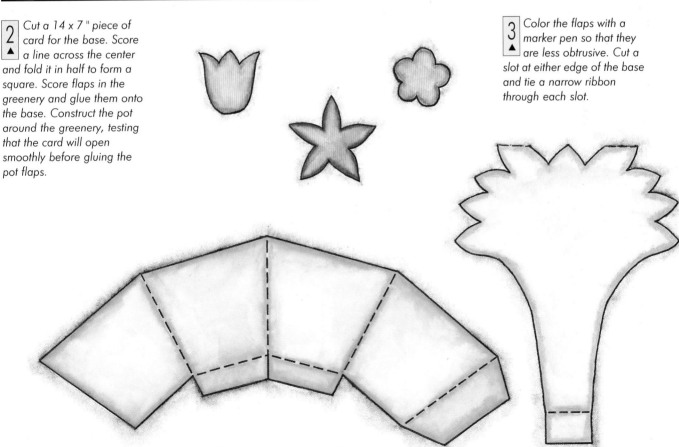

Paper Textures

Some types of paper, such as handmade paper, foil-covered paper and corrugated card, have inherently unusual textures, but an interesting texture can be added to any type of paper through the skillful use of a variety of techniques. Selectively using a range of textures within one piece can create depth, and add visual and tactile interest.

Many of the techniques which alter the natural texture of paper and card, such as embossing and paper sculpture, are covered in detail in other chapters. Other methods, such as paper pricking, crumpling, impressing, laminating, fluting, tearing, raised cutting and decorating, can enhance textures in any papercraft project. You can also make a wonderful array of objects from pre-textured materials.

Texturing techniques are particularly suitable for adding that extra dimension to pieces which would otherwise have large, flat surface areas undecorated. Varying the colors, thickness and coating of the papers or card you use with any of the texturing techniques will ensure you create finished products with flair.

Paper pricking can be done with any pointed implement. Vary the size of the holes by using different sizes, from a fine pin point, through a compass point to the point of a knitting needle. By pushing the point through the paper from the back to the front of the sheet you can create a raised surface.

Paper can be crumpled wet and then flattened until it is dry so that the flat sheet is veined with subtle creases. Alternatively paper can be crumpled dry and glued to a surface so that it remains raised on the finished piece.

When working with thicker grades of paper or card, tearing can produce a subtle contrast between the smooth surface of the paper and the rough fibers underneath.

Corrugated card and twisted ribbon are two forms of paper with a ready-made texture.

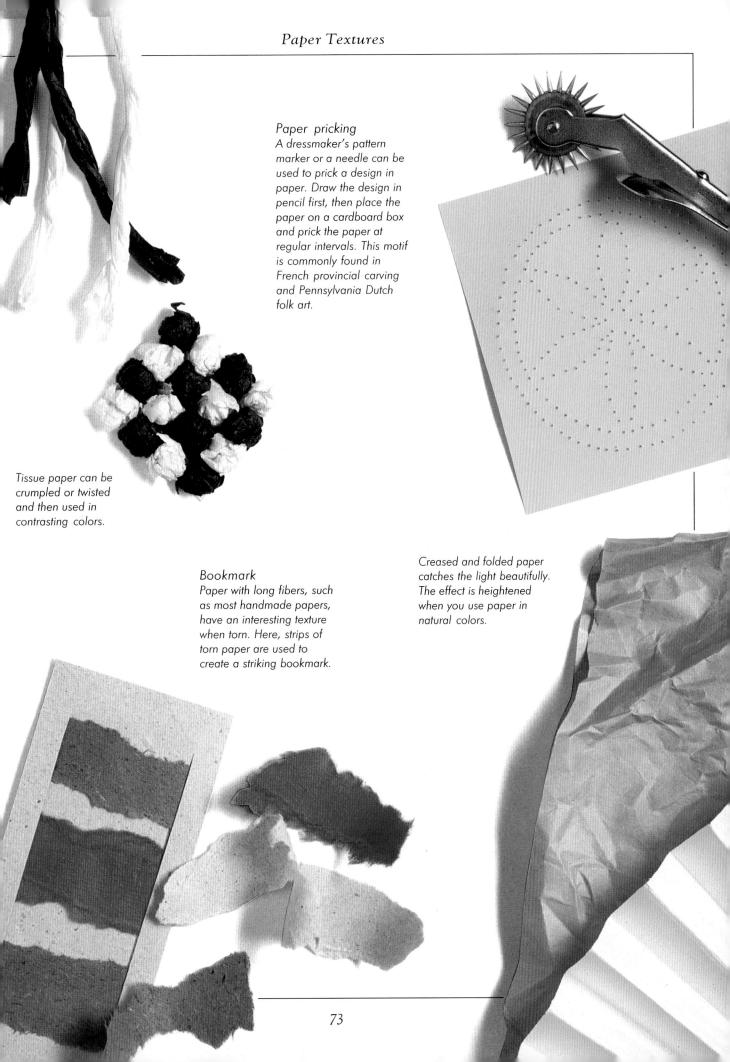

Paper pricking
A dressmaker's pattern marker or a needle can be used to prick a design in paper. Draw the design in pencil first, then place the paper on a cardboard box and prick the paper at regular intervals. This motif is commonly found in French provincial carving and Pennsylvania Dutch folk art.

Tissue paper can be crumpled or twisted and then used in contrasting colors.

Bookmark
Paper with long fibers, such as most handmade papers, have an interesting texture when torn. Here, strips of torn paper are used to create a striking bookmark.

Creased and folded paper catches the light beautifully. The effect is heightened when you use paper in natural colors.

PROJECT 22

Jeweled Crown

YOU WILL NEED
silver card
blue tissue paper
kitchen foil
tracing paper
a knife & mat
a ruler
a pencil
glue
a knitting needle

Make-believe is great entertainment, especially with a few props.
Crowns can be made in an instant and decorated with simple
slotting and crumpling techniques.

1 ▶ Cut a 21 x 5 " strip of silver card and transfer the pattern using a large knitting needle or skewer to impress the lines on the card. With a sharp knife, cut the finials and the jewel stars. Score along the dashed lines.

2 ▶ Use the knitting needle to push through the stars: pushing the top row inward and the bottom row outward. Crumple 4 " squares of blue tissue paper into balls and glue one in each of the bottom stars.

3 ▲ Glue the ends of the strip together to form a crown. Cut a 20 x 2 " strip of silver card and glue it inside to conceal the tissue balls. Cut a 20 x 6 " piece of foil, scrunch it lengthwise and glue it around the crown base.

Suggestion: Make a scepter by wrapping dowel with curling ribbon and gluing card into a slot at one end.

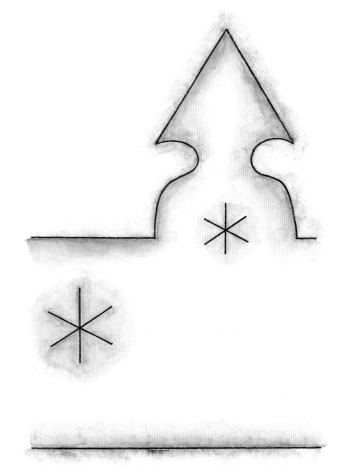

PROJECT 23

Tissue Box

Froissage is the art of pasting crumpled paper to create a transparent textured effect. In this project, it turns an everyday household item into a decorative piece.

1 ▶ Measure the height of the box of tissues and the combined width of all four sides. Allow ¹/₈ " extra on each side and cut card to those dimensions. Score the panels to fit the box. Cut another piece of card for the lid. Trace the shape of the tissue box's opening before cutting the hole.

2 ▶ Apply a coat of black paint to the sides and lid with a brush or a tin of spray paint. Using a strong adhesive, glue the side panels to form a hollow box.

3 ◀ Cut tissue wrapping paper into sheets slightly larger than each panel. Work on one panel at a time. Apply an even coverage of white glue. Crumple a sheet of tissue paper slightly and lay it over the panel, pressing it onto the glue. Complete all four panels.

4 ▶ Cover the lid in the same way. Trim and glue down any excess tissue paper. Glue the lid onto the box.

PROJECT 24

Pencil Case

YOU WILL NEED
corrugated card
black card
a knife & mat
a pencil
a ruler
scissors
glue
a paper fastener
a set of pencils

Corrugated card has an eye-catching texture as this pencil case demonstrates. When filled with high quality pencils, it will make a stylish gift for a discerning adult.

1 Cut a 9½ x 9 " piece of corrugated card, taking care not to flatten the ridges. Round the corners. Cut a 8½ x 8 " piece of black card. Cut a 1½ " slot 1 " in from a short edge. Cut a parallel slot ³/₈ " further in. Leave a gap of ¾ ", cut another pair of slots, repeat. Cut matching slots from the opposite edge.

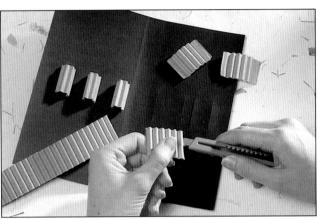

2 Cut a long strip of corrugated card 1½ " in width. Wrap it around the pencil and allow an extra ridge on each side when cutting it to length. Slice each end with a knife and flatten the outside ridges. Thread the strip through the slots in the black card. Slide a pencil into the loop to check the fit.

3 When each of the pencil loops is in position, turn the black card over and glue down the flaps. Cut a 3 x 1½ " strip of black card and round one end. In the rounded end, cut a key hole to fit the head of the paper fastener. Glue the other end beside the loop flaps.

4 Place the black card with pencils on the smooth side of the corrugated card, close the case and make a pencil mark through the keyhole on the ridged side. Insert a paper fastener and flatten the wings on the smooth side. Glue the black card section into the corrugated backing.

Printing

There are several ways in which you can apply paint or ink onto paper in a controlled manner. One is stenciling, another is printing. Once you have created a suitable design, both of these methods allow you to reproduce the image with a minimum of effort.

Relief printing is the method of copying an impression from one object and putting it onto another. It has a long history: many prehistoric people decorated their caves with handprints colored by soot or ocher.

Many "found" objects can be used in the printing process: leaves with strong outlines and vein patterns, string arranged in an interesting pattern, an apple which has been cut in half. More complex designs can be achieved by cutting into an object to create a printing block. Erasers, cork, linoleum and wood can all be carved in this way, leaving raised sections which receive the paint or ink and so print when pressed onto paper.

When designing a relief print, remember that the print will be a mirror image of your block. If your design includes lettering or a picture with a definite right and left, make sure the block image is reversed.

Small sheets of linoleum are available in most stores which sell art supplies. If using linoleum, you will also need some specialized but inexpensive cutting tools, including a straight blade, a V-shaped blade and a U-shaped one. The first is used to cut along the lines of the design and the other two to gouge linoleum from the non-printing areas. A sharp knife is adequate for carving erasers and potatoes. A pre-inked stamp pad is very handy when working with a small printing block. Larger ones will need to have paint brushed on or applied with a roller.

Printing is an ideal way of decorating a large area with a recurring motif or of making multiple copies. Personalized stationery, invitations and wrapping paper are just some of the possibilities.

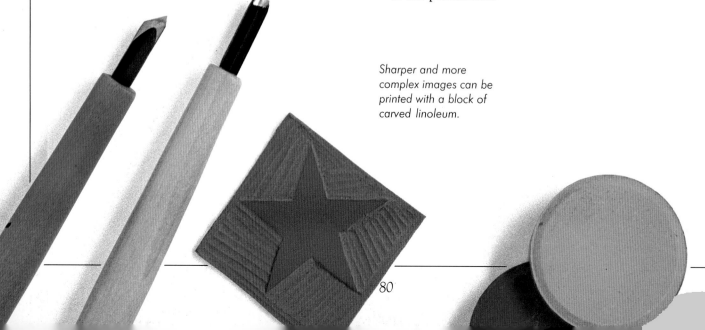

Sharper and more complex images can be printed with a block of carved linoleum.

1 Choose a suitable material to form a block such as a potato or an eraser. If using a potato, cut it in half to create a flat surface for printing. Use a sharp knife or linoleum cutting tools to carve a design; the raised area will be the printed image.

2 Apply paint to the printing block; thick paint works best. Press the block firmly onto paper, being careful not to drag it. If sections of the design do not print, you may want to modify the block. Otherwise, apply paint to the block and print again.

Before the design is cut into a block, the surface must be even, so that all the printing areas touch the paper.

If you use a square block, you can produce various patchwork patterns. Turn the block as you move it and see what arrangements are possible.

Some of the most attractive prints are imperfect images which hint at a natural shape.

PROJECT 25

Autumn Shade

YOU WILL NEED
thick paper
thin paper
a lampshade frame
acrylic paint
leaves
a brush
a pencil
a knife & mat
spray adhesive
glue

Leaf prints are one of the simplest forms of printing and one of the most attractive. Applied to a paper lampshade, they diffuse the light in a soft pattern.

1 ◀ Collect several leaves with a bold outline and veins. Brush paint mixed to a tacky consistency onto the veined side of a leaf. Place it on a large sheet of thin handmade paper and press it down with your fingers. Repeat for several prints, then discard the leaf and use a fresh one.

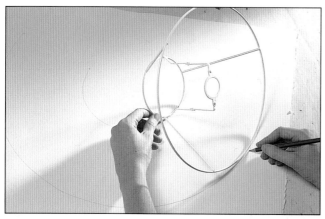

2 ◀ Lay the lampshade frame on a sheet of thick paper. Slowly roll the frame and pencil the lines of both edges to map out the shape required for the shade. Allow a 1" overlap at one end. Cut the thick paper to this shape. Cut your printed paper to the same shape but 1" larger all around.

Suggestion: If you don't have any thin handmade paper for printing on, brown parcel paper is a good substitute.

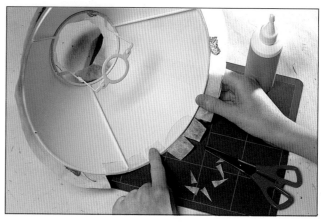

3 ◀ Wrap the thick paper around the frame and glue the overlapping end. Spray some adhesive onto the printed side of the thin paper and roll it onto the shade, making sure it lies smoothly.

4 ▶ Cut darts in the thin paper at the top and base of the shade. Place the shade on the frame, fold the darts over the wire and glue them on the inside of the shade.

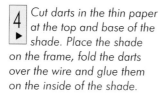

PROJECT 26

Dominoes

Dominoes are a fun game and a great help to children learning to count. This bright set is easy to make, using different colored ink pads and erasers as printing blocks.

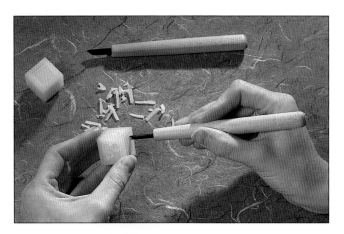

1 ▢ On one face of an eraser, draw a square ¹/₈ " in from the edge. Cut along the square with a straight blade slanting inwards. Gouge out the square, creating your "0" block. Mark a square on each face of the second eraser. Twist a U-shaped tool to cut all the circles patterns. Gouge so that the circles and border remain raised.

2 ▢ Test each face to ensure that it prints clearly. If necessary, sharpen the lines. Print a row of seven "6"s on heavy white card, inking the block each time. Below the seventh, stamp a double. Load the "5" face with a different color and print one adjoining a "6", plus six others. Continue the sequence to create 28 adjoining pairs, with a double "0" as the last.

3 ▢ While the ink is drying, cut a single raised circle on a clean face of the "0" block. This time, do not cut a border. Turn the white card over and print random dots in two colors. Print the decorative dots close together so there is no confusion which side is which.

4 ▢ Trim the dominoes with a sharp knife, cropping close to the borders. Take another piece of white card and decorate it to match the back of the dominoes. Calculate a box size to fit the dominoes; see page 154 for more information. If the set is for a young child, make a gift tag with the child's age represented in dots.

PROJECT 27

Bookplates

Bookplates are an attractive way of ensuring that favorite books come back. If this design looks a bit ambitious, you could adapt one from earlier in this chapter.

YOU WILL NEED
white paper or labels
a pencil
tracing paper
cutting tools
linoleum
printing ink
a spatula
a roller
a ruler
a knife & mat

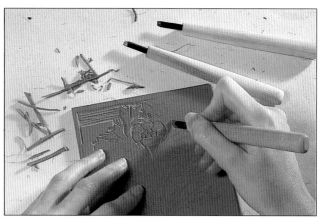

1 Trace the pattern onto tracing paper and add a name in the space at the bottom. Transfer this onto a 6 x 5 " piece of linoleum so that the pattern is reversed.

2 Cut along the lines of the design with a straight blade angled away from printing areas. Scoop out non-printing areas with a U-gouge. Work fine detail with a V-gouge.

3 Apply printing ink to the linocut and use the roller to distribute it evenly. Test the linocut by pressing it on scrap paper and recut any sections which do not print sharply. Print onto white paper or adhesive labels, checking the amount of ink and applying more when necessary. When dry, trim bookplates neatly.

Stenciling

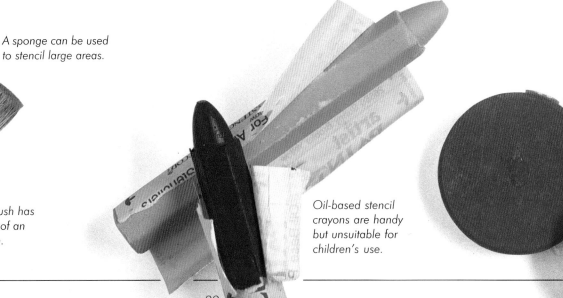

Stenciling is a relatively simple method of decorating with paint. A design is cut in card or acetate and paint is applied through this stencil, leaving an image on the surface underneath. You can buy ready-cut stencils, but it is very easy to cut your own.

When designing a stencil pattern, remember to leave "bridges" of card which hold the stencil together. This usually results in a stylized image and the best stenciled designs are often the simplest ones.

Most craft stores stock a waxed card for stencil-making and designs can be transferred onto this in pencil. However, you can also use a sheet of acetate which is available from office supplies stores. Both can be wiped clean and reused. One benefit of acetate is that you can cut the design over a tracing and position it easily when painting, a great advantage when stenciling in two or more colors.

Acrylic paints are most suitable as they dry quickly. The paint should be fairly thick so that it does not seep under the stencil and blur the design. It is also important to hold the stencil firmly in position with a removable tape and to ensure that it is lying flat against the paper.

Stenciling works on other surfaces too; the same stencils can be used to paint on fabric, wood or walls. It is also an ideal method for making many copies of a design, perhaps for an invitation or seasonal greeting cards. Stencils can be used to decorate boxes, notebooks, or even to make your own wrapping paper. If you're looking for extra inspiration, try adapting some of the other patterns in this book.

A sponge can be used to stencil large areas.

A stencil brush has stiff bristles of an even length.

Oil-based stencil crayons are handy but unsuitable for children's use.

The bridges are necessary to hold a stencil together; the challenge is to incorporate them so they form part of the design.

The cutout piece of a stencil can be useful as a reverse template.

1 Cut the design with a sharp craft knife, taking care not to slip and make unwanted cuts. Hold the blade upright so that the cut is not angled.

2 Position the stencil on the paper and tape in place. Load the brush with paint and dab any excess on scrap paper. Dab the brush down onto the stencil, working inwards from the edges of the design. Remove the stencil and wipe it clean for reuse.

PROJECT 28

Picture Cards

YOU WILL NEED
white card
adhesive paper
a pencil
a ruler
a knife & mat
acrylic paint
tracing paper
a sheet of acetate
a stencil brush
removable tape

These delightful cards are ideal for the game of concentration, played by turning cards over two at a time and trying to match pairs, or for snap. Young children will easily recognize the motifs.

1 Cover one side of thick white cardboard with a sheet of adhesive paper (or a pasted sheet of plain wrapping paper). Cut the card into twenty 2½ " squares.

2 Trace the patterns so they are well spaced. Place scrap paper under the tracing and the acetate on top. Secure the acetate with tape. With a cutting mat underneath, use a sharp knife to cut out the shapes.

3 Position the stencil over a card. Load the brush with paint and dab off excess. Paint with a stippling action, taking care that no paint seeps under the stencil. Mask off areas to be painted in a different color using removable tape. Paint each design on two squares to produce ten pairs of cards.

PROJECT 29

Menu Scrolls

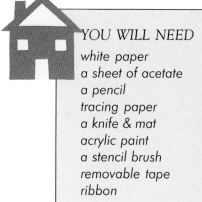

YOU WILL NEED
white paper
a sheet of acetate
a pencil
tracing paper
a knife & mat
acrylic paint
a stencil brush
removable tape
ribbon

A handwritten menu adds a stylish touch to a meal, whether it be Christmas or just a special dinner party. To ensure a clean finish, a stencil is cut for each color of the design.

1 | Trace the pattern and rule a line alongside it, ¾ " apart. Place the tracing on a sheet of scrap paper. Position the acetate on top, so that the edge lies on the ruled line and secure with tape. With a mat underneath, cut out the berries. Rotate the acetate, line it up again, and cut out the leaves and stem.

2 | Cut paper into sheets 6½ x 9 " (or use pre-cut sheets of writing paper). Tape the stencil to a sheet. Load the brush with green paint and dab any excess on scrap paper. Paint the leaves and stems with a stippling action, making sure no paint seeps under the stencil.

Suggestion: Stencil the design on card or stiff paper to make matching place cards.

3 | When the first color is dry, rotate the stencil and paint the berries in the same way. Allow to dry. With a calligraphy or fountain pen, write the menu below the design. Roll each menu and tie with a ribbon.

PROJECT 30

Photo Album

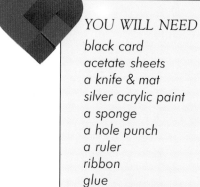

Photographs are full of treasured memories and a homemade album provides the setting they deserve. The stenciled border is applied with a sponge and can be flipped to fit any corner.

YOU WILL NEED
black card
acetate sheets
a knife & mat
silver acrylic paint
a sponge
a hole punch
a ruler
ribbon
glue
double-sided tape

1 Cut thin black card into twenty-two rectangles measuring 12 x 9 ". Cut two sheets of acetate to match. Cut two 1½ x 9 " strips of black card for the spine of the front and back covers.

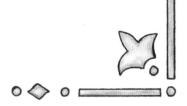

2 Trace the pattern and place the tracing on scrap paper. Place the acetate on top and secure it to the tracing with tape then cut out the shapes. Position the stencil on the black card and sponge a small amount of silver paint onto the design area. Repeat on other pages, stenciling the design in different corners.

3 Stencil a title box on a blank piece of card. Cut a 9 " strip of double-sided tape and use it to attach a sheet of acetate. Use more tape to then attach a spine strip, forming a front cover. Attach acetate and a spine strip to a plain piece of card to form a back cover.

Suggestion: If you know the dimension of the photographs, you can also stencil around the corners.

4 Punch two holes along the spine of the back cover and thread a piece of ribbon through. Punch holes likewise in each page and thread onto the ribbon, adding some glue between the holes for extra strength. Holepunch the front cover, add it to the stack and tie the ribbon in a tight bow.

Marbling

Marbling, so called because the swirls of paint can sometimes resemble the veins of marbled stone, has been a highly prized skill throughout its history.

In Japan, paper decorated by floating ink on water in a technique called *suminagashi* was reserved for the imperial household. The Turks thickened water with gum and called their marbling *ebru* or cloud art. The technique was guarded as a state secret by the Ottomans who used marbled papers for important documents. When marbling reached Europe in the sixteenth century, the commercial value of marbled paper encouraged craftsmen to control its production. They cunningly trained their apprentices in only one aspect of the craft, creating a source of cheap but uninformed labor.

Today, marbled effects can be achieved using various combinations of paint and size. The simplest of these is oil-on-water which is inexpensive and quick. The only drawback is that you have little control over the paint and can create only simple designs. The kite (Project 31) demonstrates this method.

By using a thicker size, the marbler gains greater control. A good compromise is to float oil paint on a thin wallpaper paste. You can then manipulate the paint using combs and skewers to replicate some of the classic marbling patterns.

Carrageen-and-watercolor is the most complicated of the three methods but allows the marbler to create very precise patterns. The complications lie in the preparation. The size must be prepared by blending carrageen with water. This is allowed to stand for twelve hours, then skimmed with a strip of newspaper. Paper must be treated with a "mordant", a chemical that fixes colors, by dipping it in a bath of alum solution and allowing it to dry before marbling. The watercolors must be mixed with ox gall to encourage them to float rather than sink. All this activity is fully rewarded by the results you can then achieve.

However it is created, paper which has been marbled should be put to decorative use: covering books, boxes, lampshades, picture frames and anything else deserving attention.

Make your own combs and rakes by clamping sewing pins between two strips of card, secured with double-sided tape. A rake's teeth are spaced more widely than those of a comb.

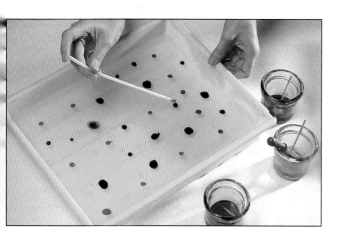 

1 Prepare the size and allow it to rest in a deep tray. Cut the paper to fit the tray and mordant it if marbling on carrageen. Prepare the paints, thinning oil paints with turpentine or adding ox gall to watercolors. Skim the size with a strip of newspaper to break the surface tension. Spatter the paint onto the size with straws, eye droppers or a whisk. Use a skewer, rake or comb to create your pattern.

2 Lay the paper on the size, ensuring that no bubbles of air are trapped under it. Lift the paper off and rinse it under a cold tap. Skim any remaining paint from the size with paper strips and repeat the process with your next piece of paper.

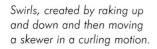

Even the smallest scraps of marbled paper can be used to create beautiful objects, such as earrings or coiled beads.

Swirls, created by raking up and down and then moving a skewer in a curling motion.

A nonpareil design, made by raking up and down, side to side and then combing down.

A get gel pattern, formed by raking from side to side and then up and down.

 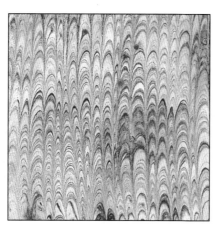 

PROJECT 31

Swirling Kite

This beautiful kite is decorated with simple oil-on-water marbling. It is an ideal project for adults and children to make and use together.

YOU WILL NEED
white paper
drinking straws
oil paints
turpentine
wooden skewers
¼ " dowel
a drill
glue
a knife & mat
string & ribbon
a curtain ring

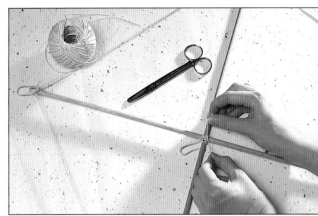

1 ▲ Fill a tray with water. Thin oil paints with turpentine. Use a bundle of straws to spatter paint onto the water. Swirl paint with a skewer and lay a large sheet of paper on top. Lift the paper and lay it on newspaper to dry. Ten or so 16½ x 15½ " sheets are required.

2 ▲ Cut two lengths (one at 33½ " and the other 25 ") of ¼ " dowel. Drill a small hole in each end of the dowels. Bind them into a cross with the horizontal bar one-third down the vertical bar. Thread string through each of the holes and tie it taut. Attach string loops at the top, bottom and center of the frame.

3 ▶ Glue pieces of marbled paper together to form a large sheet. Lay the kite frame on top and cut around it, allowing a ¾ " margin at each edge. Angle the corners so that the edges can be folded over the string and glued down. The paper should be taut.

4 ▶ Cut a small hole in the marbled paper and pull the string loop through. Cut 5 ' of ribbon. Attach one end to the center loop and the other end to the top loop. Knot a curtain ring in the middle as shown and tie the kite string to it. This bridle may need to be adjusted when you fly the kite.

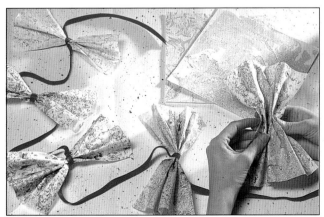

5 ◀ Cut a 12 ' length of ribbon for the tail. Cut marbled paper into 8 " squares. Gather each sheet at the center and tie them onto the ribbon at 10 " intervals. Tie the tail onto the loop at the base of the kite frame.

PROJECT 32

Placemats

Beautiful marbling deserves to be framed and, when turned into placemats, can be admired by everyone. The designs in this project are marbled on a wallpaper size.

YOU WILL NEED
white paper
thick card
colored card
wallpaper paste
marbling equipment
oil paints
mineral turpentine
double-sided tape
a knife & mat
a ruler
acrylic varnish

1 ▶ *Mix a size from wallpaper paste (see page 97) and pour into a deep tray. Cut sheets of white paper to fit the tray, but at least 12 x 10 ". Dilute oil paints with mineral turpentine and scatter drops on the size. Form patterns with a skewer or comb and lay paper on the size. Lift the paper and wash off any size under a cold tap.*

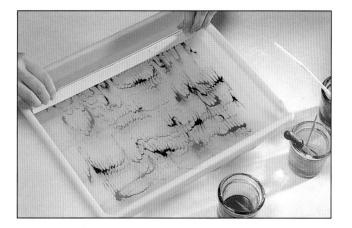

2 ▶ *Prepare a frame for the placemat by cutting a 12 x 10 " piece of colored card. Measure 1 " in from each edge and cut out a rectangle to create a 1 " frame. Cut a 12 x 10 " piece of thick backing card.*

Suggestion: With the scraps of colored card and marbled paper, make a set of matching napkin rings.

3 ◀ *Decide which is the best area of the marbled paper and crop it down to 11½ x 9½ ". Apply double-sided tape around the back of the frame and stick it over the marbled paper.*

4 ▶ *Apply a coat of acrylic varnish to the framed marbling. Arrange strips of double-sided tape around the edges of the backing card and in the center. Align the framed marbling and press it smoothly onto the backing card. Use these instructions to make a complete set of mats.*

PROJECT 33

Bookmarks

Classic marbling techniques are traditionally associated with bookbinding, so what better way to use up precious scraps of marbled paper than by making an elegant bookmark?

YOU WILL NEED
white paper
marbling equipment
alum
carrageen size
marbling paints
a ruler
a knife & mat
glue
embroidery cotton
gold thread

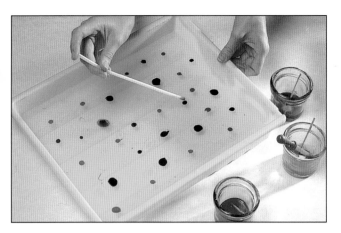

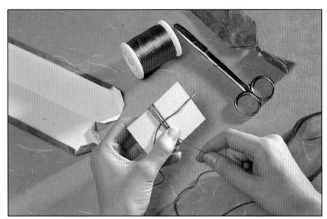

1 ▲ Make the size and allow it to sit for 12 hours. Mordant the paper and let it dry. Mix the paints and skim the size. Apply the paint and comb it into a pattern. Lay the paper on the size, then lift it off and rinse it under a cold tap. For more information on these techniques see pages 96-97.

2 ▲ Enlarge the pattern below by 125% and transfer it onto the marbled paper. Fold along the center line and then fold the end flaps and side flaps.

3 ◄ Lay 2 " of embroidery thread across a piece of card and then wind more thread around the card. Slip this off the card and bind one end with gold thread. Trim the ends to form a tassel. Glue the 2 " guide thread inside the end flaps. Apply glue to the end and side flaps, fold and press the bookmark flat.

Paper Appliqué

Appliqué is the term used to describe the craft of sewing cutout pieces of fabric onto a backing material to create a lifelike scene or a decorative pattern. Paper appliqué uses the same basic techniques of cutting and combining pieces to form an attractive design. It shares some of the characteristics and techniques of both découpage and papercutting.

Many cultures have long standing folk traditions involving the cutting and pasting of paper. Throughout Europe, various countries have gradually developed distinctive styles of working with fragments of paper to create ornamental pieces.

The Polish tradition of cutting and combining paper pieces, *wycinanki*, includes several diverse regional styles. Some of these use a single color of paper with a contrasting background. *Kodry* employs a brilliant array of colors to make enchanting pictorial collages. Carefully shaped pieces are positioned, side-by-side on a background with no gaps between them, to portray complex scenes, such as guests seated at a wedding banquet. *Lowicz*, named after its area of origin in Poland,

is a style which involves layering colored pieces on the background to form images with greater depth.

The projects in this chapter use techniques ranging from simple cutting, pasting and layering of paper shapes to adorn a lively collection of spinning tops, and an elegant flower press, through to the more advanced shaping and classical design of a mosaic, where the spaces between the pieces are as much a part of the design as the paper tiles themselves.

In any paper appliqué project, the design should be laid out with care before the glue is applied, to ensure that all your cut pieces will fit together to form an appealing and cohesive image. Choose paper or card of a color, thickness and surface texture which will enhance the finished piece.

For the projects in this chapter you can use a sharp knife and a small pair of scissors to cut and shape the pieces, unlike the Poles who, during an era when all scissors and sharp knives were confiscated by the ruling authorities, continued making their intricate papercuts using the tips of large and unwieldy sheep shears!

Lowicz bird
The birds depicted in this region of Poland include roosters, peacocks and doves. Cut your base shape out of black paper. Place it on colored paper and trace around it, then cut a shape from within the tracing. Place this shape on another color of paper, trace around it and so on. These shapes are then glued in layers.

Nightscape
This dramatic frame illustrates the difference between papercutting and paper appliqué. Here, the moons and stars have been cut from silver card and glued onto black card. A very similar effect could be gained by cutting out the shapes in the black frame and backing it with strips of silver card.

Paper glass
Black card can be cut and backed with colored tissue paper or cellophane to create the impression of leaded glass. If you seal the tissue between two identical black sections, the piece can be hung in a window to catch the light.

PROJECT 34

Spinning Tops

Tops hold a great fascination for young children and here are a whole troupe of brightly colored examples. The colors change when the tops are spun, especially those of the rainbow one.

YOU WILL NEED
white card
colored card
a compass
a pencil
scissors
glue
dowel
a pencil sharpener

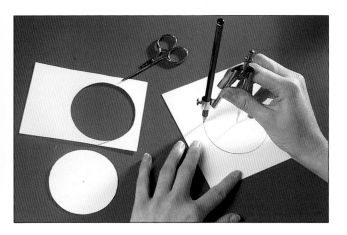

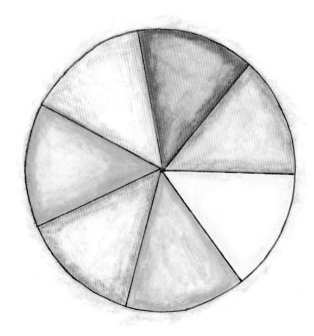

1 ▲ Use a compass to draw circles with a diameter of 3 " on white card. Cut out each circle with scissors. It is easy to make several tops at the one time.

Suggestion: The gift box is a triangular version of a lidded box with a folded divider glued inside.

2 ◄ Cut shapes from colored card and glue them onto the circles. For the rainbow top, cut seven equal segments using the pattern above. For the spotted top, cut triangles and squares from colored strips and use a hole punch to cut circles.

3 ▼ Cut a piece of ¼ " dowel into 3 " lengths. Use a pencil sharpener to create a point, but do not make them dangerously sharp, especially if the tops are for young children. Pierce the circles with the dowels.

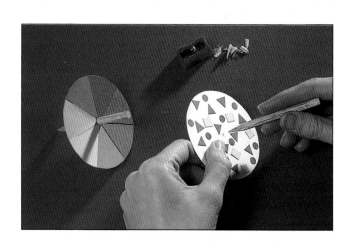

Flower Press

Pressed flowers make beautiful cards and petals are invaluable for papermaking. The press itself can be an object of distinction with a circlet of paper flowers appliquéd on the top.

YOU WILL NEED
plywood
blotting paper
cardboard
colored card
masking tape & glue
tracing paper
pencil & ruler
a drill
a knife & mat
bolts & wing nuts

1 Cut two 6 x 8 " rectangles of sturdy ply. Tape them together and make a pencil mark in each corner, ¾ " in from the edge. With a piece of scrap timber underneath, drill holes to match your bolt size.

2 Transfer the pattern onto colored paper or card and cut out shapes with small scissors or a sharp knife. Use a hole punch to create the flower centers.

3 Assemble six flowers and six leaves with glue. Arrange them in a circle on a piece of ply. Glue in place one at a time.

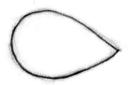

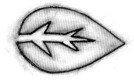

4 Cut rectangles of blotting paper and cardboard 5½ x 7½ " in size. Use a ruler or a 45 degree triangle to cut off corners. Assemble the press, with two sheets of blotting paper between each piece of cardboard, and secure the bolts with wing nuts on the top.

PROJECT 36

Mosaic Tile

The use of colored chips to build up a larger picture is put to good effect in this decorative tile. It features two carp, a Chinese symbol of good fortune.

YOU WILL NEED
thick white card
colored card
tracing paper
a pencil & eraser
a compass
scissors
a knife & mat
a toothpick
glue
a brush
acrylic varnish

1 On heavy white card, draw a circle 10 " in diameter. Transfer the fish pattern twice, flipping it so that the two fish face each other. Use the tracing to cut the large sections of the fish from gold card. Cut the scales with a sharp knife. Using scissors, cut strips of blue and green card and then snip these into small chips.

2 Paste down the large fish parts and then the scales, erasing pencil lines as you work. Use a toothpick to dab glue onto the back of each chip. Paste down chips of blue and green card to form concentric circles. Chips in the center must be trimmed at an angle before gluing. You will also need to trim those adjacent to the fish.

3 Cut out the circle of white card and apply several coats of acrylic varnish to protect the tile. Attach wire to the back if you wish to hang it on a wall.

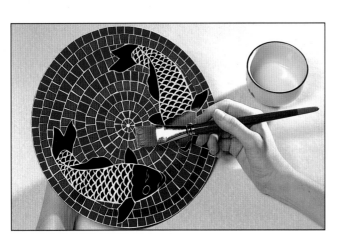

Quilling

There is something curious about cutting a piece of paper into long strips, rolling them into different shapes and combining them to form elaborate designs. Curious or not, quilling is now and has long been a popular pastime. It began as an inexpensive imitation of gold and silver filigree decoration commissioned by medieval churches which could not afford the precious metals. Centuries on, it was revived by the women of the Victorian era who prized it as a demonstration of skill and patience.

Patience is definitely one of the virtues required: quilling is not a craft for anyone who wants to produce instant results. A certain dexterity of the fingers is also necessary, although the paper strips can be cut to any width which suits the quiller. If both patience and dexterity are in ample supply, the results can be most rewarding and surprisingly beautiful.

Quilling strips are sold in many craft stores but if you cannot source any, it is quite easy to cut your own. Choose a good quality paper which will hold a shape when rolled and that is available in a range of colors. With a sharp craft knife and a metal ruler, cut in the direction of the grain to create strips ¼ " wide. Most shapes require strips that are between 2 and 6 " in length.

The size of the quilling tool used to roll the strips will determine the size of the hole in the center of your quilled shape. A wooden cocktail stick or a bent paper clip is ideal. There are two types of quilled shape: closed forms or coils, which are held in shape with glue, and scrolls, which are open forms with a looser shape. The directory on the next page shows the variation that can be achieved.

Once you have formed the quilling shapes, they can be arranged in a pattern and glued in place. If the design is a complex one, work on thick cardboard and use pins to hold the pieces in position. Quilling can be used to decorate anything from greeting cards to boxes and frames.

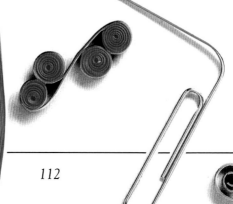

Roll strips around a cocktail stick, a large paper clip or a bought quilling tool.

Tight coil
Glue the end of the strip to prevent it unwinding.

Off-center coil
Use a pin to pull the center of a loose coil, then glue to one side.

Loose scroll
Allow coil to spring open and remain unglued.

Loose coil
Allow coil to unwind before gluing the end.

Triangle
Gently pinch three corners of a loose coil.

S-scroll
Roll a strip half-way; turn, roll the other end.

Eye
Evenly pinch opposite sides of a loose coil.

Crescent
Pinch a loose coil twice to form a concave line.

Kite
Make a petal and pinch three extra points.

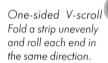

Heart
Fold strip in half and roll each end inwards.

Teardrop
Pinch a loose coil to form a point.

Petal
Bend the point of a teardrop to one side.

V-scroll
Fold strip in half and roll each end outwards.

Diamond
Make an eye and pinch two extra points.

Leaf
Twist the points of an eye.

One-sided V-scroll
Fold a strip unevenly and roll each end in the same direction.

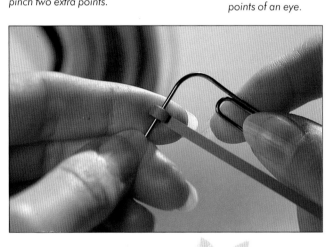

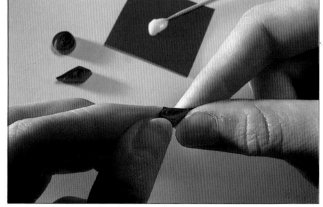

1 ▲ Cut paper strips to length, as indicated beside the pattern. To start coiling, wind the end of a strip tightly around your quilling tool. Use one hand to turn the quilling tool towards you and the other to guide the paper. Maintain an even tension until the end of the strip.

2 ▲ Release the coil, slip it off the end of the quilling tool and let it unwind until it reaches the size you want. For closed coils, dab glue on the inside edge and press closed. Finally, pinch the coil to the desired shape.

A circle template is useful for forming coils of a uniform size.

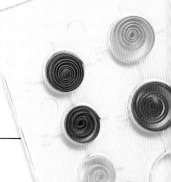

PROJECT 37

Butterfly Mobile

YOU WILL NEED
cocktail sticks
glue
ruler
a knife & mat
scissors
colored paper
wooden skewers
clear thread
double-sided tape

This bright mobile is quilled with wide strips of paper which makes it a suitable project for novices or children. Test that the paper will roll smoothly before cutting all the strips.

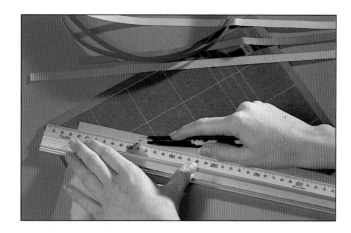

1 ◀ Cut strong paper into strips ³/₈ " wide, cutting in the direction of the paper grain. The wings of each butterfly require two shades of a color and all the bodies are a dark green or black. Cut strips to the lengths indicated below.

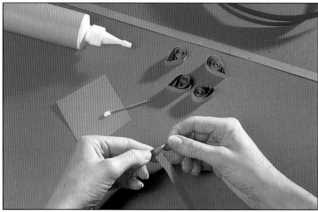

For each butterfly
One 4 " V-scroll
One 3 " tight coil
One 6 " crescent
One 8 " crescent
Two 18 " tears
Two 12 " tears

2 ▲ Use a cocktail stick or other quilling tool to roll each strip. Refer to page 113, which explains how to form each shape. Arrange the quilled pieces on a flat surface and glue the shapes together.

3 ▶ Wind paper strips around two wooden skewers and secure the ends with double-sided tape. Glue the skewers to form a crossbar. Attach clear thread to form a loop for hanging. Tie a thread to each butterfly and attach them to the crossbar, testing the mobile for balance.

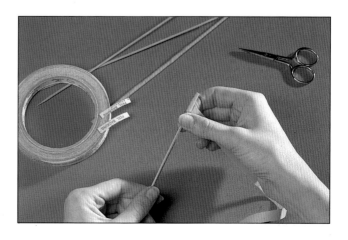

PROJECT 38

Quilled Jewelry

The sun, the moon and the stars seem a suitable gift for a special friend. You should be able to buy the jewelry fittings needed for this delicate project from most craft stores.

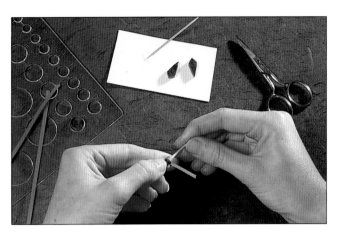

Fiery sun brooch
One 16 " loose coil
Seven 6 " triangles
Seven 8 " kites
with an added twist

1 ▲ Cut paper strips to length, as indicated beside the pattern. Use a cocktail stick or other quilling tool to roll each strip. Refer to page 113, which explains how to form each shape. Where it is important to create shapes of a consistent size (such as the star) fit loose coils in a circle template before shaping.

Starry earrings
Ten 9 " kites

Twin moon earrings
Two 16 " crescent
Four grey 2 " tight coils
Ten white 2 " tight coils

2 ◄ To form the star, apply glue to the short sides of each kite and fix in place. Glue the orange triangles onto the yellow sun coil and add the twisted kites, making the flames point in the same direction. To assemble the moon, form a triangle of tight coils and glue the tip of the crescent into a gap. Glue four tight coils to form a tube.

3 ► Attach jewelry fittings. Cut a disk of gold card and glue it onto the brooch backing, then glue on the sun. Loop fine wire through an earring wire, the tube of coils and the moon section, then thread it back though the tube. Use jump rings to connect the stars to earring wires, or glue to clip-on mounts.

Suggestion: For extra strength, apply a coat of acrylic varnish to the quilled pieces.

PROJECT 39

Tree Decorations

YOU WILL NEED
cocktail sticks
glue
a ruler
scissors
colored paper strips
ribbon
a circle template
a compass
thick cardboard
pins

Quilled ornaments will add a beautiful touch to Christmas festivities. If making them as a gift, add a small quilled motif to the box.

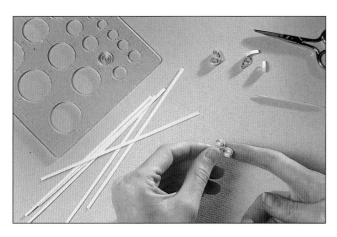

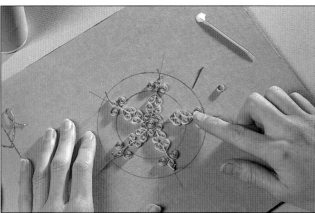

1 ◄ Cut paper strips to length, as indicated beside the pattern. Use a cocktail stick or other quilling tool to roll strips. Refer to page 113 to form shapes. For accurate sizing, fit coils in a circle template before shaping.

Christmas tree
Two 3 " V-scrolls
Four 4 " V-scrolls
Three 5 " V-scrolls
Ten 4 " open coils
Two 6 " open coils
Four 6 " one-sided
  V-scrolls
Seven 2 " tight coils
One 2 " tight coil

2 ▲ Arrange quilled pieces on a flat surface and glue any adjoining sections. For circular designs, draw concentric circles on card with a compass and position the sections on this guide. Cut ribbon in 4 " lengths and tie through the loop.

Snowflake
Five 6 " eyes
Five 6 " tears
Five 6 " V-scrolls
One 2 " tight coil

Christmas star
One 8 " loose coil
Five 2 " loose coils
Twenty 4½ " tears
Five 6 " V-scrolls
Five 4 " tears
One 2 " tight coil

Holly wreath
Twenty-four 3 " tight coils
Twenty-four 6 " diamonds
One 2 " tight coil

Paper Sculpture

Sculpture is generally considered to be one of the "fine arts" and the creation of forms with paper produces results as fine as other types of sculpture. With a few basic techniques, the unique qualities of the medium can be exploited to produce pieces which have a great strength and formal beauty.

Paper sculpture can take one of two forms: relief (which is slightly raised but designed to be viewed front-on) or fully three-dimensional. Classic paper sculpture is worked in white only, allowing the light to emphasize subtle curves and folds. The same effect, however, can be achieved with paper in a single color. When using colored card or paper, make sure that the dye goes right through as scored lines will reveal the core of the paper. Choose a paper that will retain a shape: cartridge paper is a good

starting point but you can experiment with other weights and textures. You will also need a quick-drying clear glue or double-sided tape for fixing segments together.

Before embarking on a major project, practice scoring lines and creasing folds. The amount of pressure required will depend on the sharpness of your blade. If the paper does not score smoothly, replace the blade.

The subject matter is only limited by your imagination. Figures can be constructed with cones and cylinders and then decorated with additional pieces. Two of the three projects in this chapter are classic stylized designs worked in relief which is a relatively simple but effective method.

When folded, paper gains extra strength. However, a paper sculpture is a relatively fragile work of art and should be admired rather than used.

The equipment needed to sculpt paper is minimal.

Variations
Four disks decorated with curved score lines. The top left has been cut and the edges overlapped to form a cone, reducing the size slightly.

1 Plan your design with a pencil before cutting it out with a sharp craft knife. Score any fold lines lightly, breaking the surface of the paper but taking care not to cut completely through.

2 Holding the piece, gently pinch the score lines and ease each fold into shape. Some forms can be pulled and held in place with glue or tape.

Stiff paper is well-suited for stylized designs and figures. For a more natural effect, use a flexible paper, such as crêpe paper.

PROJECT 40

Sun Mask

This regal sun mask shows what can be achieved with quite simple relief sculpture. It will make a perfect companion for anyone attending a fancy dress party or a masked ball.

1 ▶ *Enlarge the pattern to 225% and transfer it onto gold card using tracing paper and a pencil. Cut out all the pieces and cut the holes for the eyes. Lightly score all the dashed lines. Note that the lines of the lips must be scored on the back.*

2 ▶ *Cut a 16" length of dowel. Cut a narrow strip of double-sided tape and stick it along one side of the dowel. Wrap gold-colored ribbon tightly around the dowel. Attach the dowel to the back of the sun with strong adhesive tape.*

3 ▲ *Gently mold the scored lines with your fingertips, raising the rays, nose and eyebrow pieces, and inverting the mouth. Roll strips of double-sided tape into wads and use these to attach the facial features to the mask.*

Suggestion: Foil-covered card can be difficult to shape: you could use plain card and spray it gold afterwards.

PROJECT 41

Coat of Arms

The pomp and splendor of medieval heraldry can be recaptured with a classic fleur-de-lis relief. Better still, use the principles of paper sculpture to devise your own design.

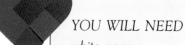

1 Transfer the fleur-de-lis and star patterns onto blue paper. Cut out the pieces and score the broken lines: note that the dashed lines are scored on the front, the dotted lines at the back. Gently shape the pieces.

2 Cut a 11½ x 7 " piece of stiff white paper. Score a series of lines across it, at ¾ " intervals. Turn the sheet over and repeat, scoring lines between those already scored on the reverse. Fold back and forth in a series of reverse folds to form a background.

3 Enlarge the shield pattern to 300%, transfer it onto blue paper and cut out. Trim the white background to fit the shield. Glue the shield tabs to frame the background. Cut and attach a backing sheet with a small hole for hanging. Use double-sided tape to attach the stars and fleur-de-lis to the front.

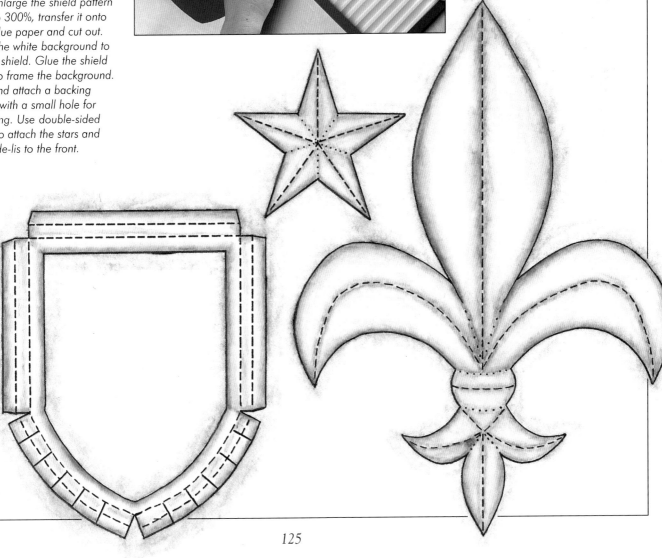

PROJECT 42

Wreath of Roses

YOU WILL NEED
crêpe paper
scissors
wire
double-sided tape
wreath base
ribbon

This romantic wreath shows the potential of paper to form fully rounded shapes. Crêpe paper won't survive the rain or damp, so it should be hung indoors or under shelter.

1 ▲ Cut and pleat a 12" strip of red crêpe paper to form eight layers. Cut a petal shape, leaving the sides uncut to create a chain of petals. Separate the last two petals. Cut green sepals. Curl sepals and petal tops, drawing them over a blade. Stretch each petal as shown.

2 ▲ Pierce the petal base with a wire, then twist the wire to secure. Wrap the petal chain around quite tightly, gathering each one at the base. Add the spare petals, allowing them to curl open. Secure at the base with tape.

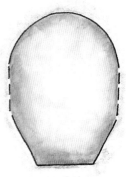

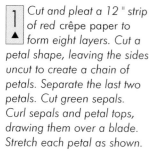

3 ◄ Cut a narrow green strip for the stem. Wrap the sepals around the base. Attach the stem strip and wind it carefully around the wire. Secure with tape. Cut green leaves and secure each one to a wire, then wrap the wire with a stem strip and fasten with a piece of tape.

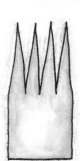

4 ► Bind the wreath base with green ribbon. Insert the roses and leaves so that they all point in the same direction. Make a separate bow from the ribbon and attach it with wire.

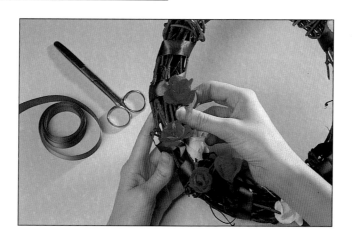

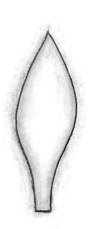

Covering

Within the last decade or so, the range of printed giftwraps available has improved dramatically, to the point where there is now a dazzling choice. Some designs are so attractive that it seems a pity to see them simply torn apart by an over-excited birthday celebrant. You might give such papers a longer life, using them to transform worn out objects or items which were decorated in an out-of-date style.

There are two possibilities when decorating with giftwrap. One is that you have a particular project in mind: an item to be made in heavy-duty card or an old piece which needs rejuvenating. The other possibility is that a particular giftwrap catches your eye.

If so, let the design inspire you. A delicate floral pattern, for example, may suit a purpose which a bright children's design would not. When choosing a paper for covering, consider the color, strength and size of the sheet and also whether you will need to align a complex pattern at the edges.

Some papers are subject to shrinking and stretching and it is wise to test a small piece by dampening it before using it on a major project. Always determine the grain and use this to advantage (see pages 12-13). It may be worthwhile sealing thin papers by spraying a coat of acrylic sealer on the printed side. Another method of conserving and strengthening giftwrap is to laminate it with clear self-adhesive plastic.

Every house is filled with objects waiting to be covered. Waste paper baskets, notebooks and albums, blotters, lampshades and boxes of all shapes and sizes can be beautifully decorated in this way.

Lacquerwork
A box made of plain card becomes a treasure when covered with a suitable giftwrap and given several coats of polyurethane varnish. Black and dark colors work best with this treatment, but take care to keep the piece free of dust when varnishing.

◄ Empty matchboxes can be used to make various pieces of furniture in miniature. These ones have been covered with an adhesive contact.

► Turn matchboxes into a decorator item. Cover two squares of card with decorative paper. Glue four matchboxes to the base so that each one opens in a different direction and there is a gap in the centre. Glue on the cover and attach a paper fastener to each drawer.

Quick covering
Self-adhesive plastic covering is available in a range of bright colors and decorative patterns. It is durable and, in some projects, easier to apply than glued papers.

PROJECT 43

Baby Kit

YOU WILL NEED

thick card
tracing paper
a pencil
giftwrap
white paper
a knife & mat
a ruler
glue
spray adhesive

Brighten the baby's room with these useful hexagonal containers. A single sheet of giftwrap will cover several boxes, which can be sized to suit your needs.

1 ▲ Cut out a 11 x 2¼ " strip of thick card. Score six lines to form seven panels of equal size. Cut a ³/₈ " strip from the last panel and peel a layer of paper off to create an end flap. Transfer the hexagon pattern onto card and cut out the base.

2 ▶ Glue the side panels to form a hexagon, overlapping the end flap onto the first panel. Insert the base, making sure that it fits snugly, and glue around the join.

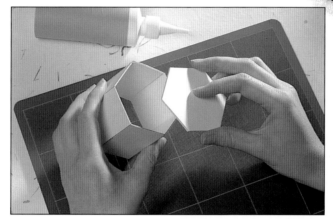

3 ▶ Cut a 10¼ x 3 " piece of giftwrap. Apply a coat of spray adhesive to the undecorated side and place the box at one end. Working on one panel at a time, snip the giftwrap so the edges can be folded onto the base or tucked into the box.

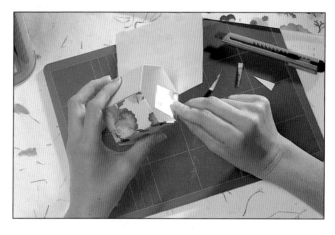

4 ◀ Make sure all the flaps are securely glued down. Cut a hexagon of giftwrap and cover the base with it. Cut a 10 x 2¹/₈ " piece of white paper. Insert it in the box and use your fingers to mold it into the corners. Remove the paper, apply spray adhesive and paste it inside the box.

Suggestion: Dimensions have been given for the smallest box. The other boxes in the picture have a panel size of 4½ x 2¼ " and 6 x 3 ". Enlarge the hexagon pattern so that each edge matches the panel width.

PROJECT 44

Crackers

YOU WILL NEED

crêpe paper
thin white paper
cardboard tubes
cracker snaps
scissors
a knife & mat
curling ribbon
gold stars
balloons
small treats

Crackers are great fun on any special occasion, particularly when they contain a personalized rhyme or riddle. Red crackers with a green band look festive on the Christmas table.

1 ▶ To make party hats for the crackers, cut a 6 x 24 " piece of crêpe paper and fold it in two. Cut a zigzag pattern along one long edge, then glue the ends to form a crown. Write a riddle or rhyme on a small slip of white paper and fold it.

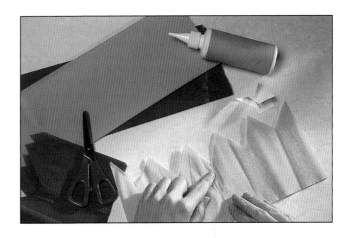

2 ▶ Cut a 12 x 9 " piece of crêpe paper and place a 10 x 8 " piece of thin white paper on top. Glue the two together at the long edge nearest you. Place a cracker snap on top of this.

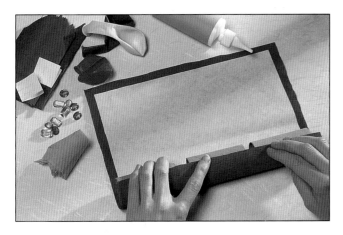

3 ◀ Cut a 3 " length of cardboard tube and insert a party hat, balloon, motto and a small gift. Place the tube over the snap and lay another tube at either end to support the shape. Roll the cracker tightly and secure the crêpe paper with a dab of glue.

4 ▶ Tie each end with curling ribbon and then remove the support tubes. Cut a 8 x 1½ " strip of crêpe paper in a contrasting color and roll it around the cracker as a decorative collar, securing it with glue. Stick a gold star on the front of the cracker.

PROJECT 45

Desk Set

A pencil holder and note box are invaluable for the student's desktop or for that spot beside the telephone where there's never a pencil and paper when you need them.

YOU WILL NEED
thick card
black card
giftwrap
a cardboard tube
pencils & a notepad
glue
spray adhesive
a ruler
a knife & mat
double-sided tape

1 For the note box, enlarge the patterns by 200% and cut these shapes in thick card. Score the dashed lines, fold and glue the corners. Cut two pieces of giftwrap: one 8 x 4¾ " and another 10 x 9 ". Spray adhesive on the unpatterned side and cover the two box sections, cutting darts where appropriate. Glue the two sections together.

2 For the pot, cut a 4 " length of tube. Cut a disk of thick card for the base and glue it to the tube. Roll giftwrap around it and glue the edge. Cut darts in each end, tuck them over and glue down. Cover the base with a disk of giftwrap. Insert some black card to cover the darts.

3 To wrap pencils, cut strips of giftwrap 1½ " wide and the same length as the pencil. Roll the pencil in it and secure with a strip of double-sided tape.

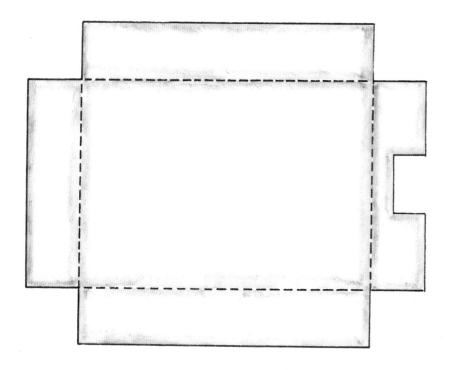

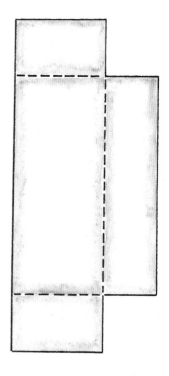

Folding

One of the properties of paper is that it can be folded and a crisp fold is a source of delight to the eye. This property can be exploited to great effect and in various ways, some of which are explored in this chapter.

Soon after knowledge of the papermaking process reached Japan, the Japanese developed a style of paper folding known as origami. This art form is a very exact one with two rules: the paper must be a square sheet and nothing can be added or cut away from this shape. Within these parameters, there is great scope for ingenuity and inventiveness. Origami has attracted much interest from Westerners in the last fifty or so years and there are many excellent books specifically on this topic.

Traditional origami designs represent birds, animals and flowers. Some of these have moving parts, others are purely ornamental. There are also many designs for boxes, although the strength of the paper limits their functional use.

On the whole, origami should be approached as a relaxing and enjoyable pastime and a springboard for creative thought rather than as a practical craft.

Taking a wider approach to the folding of paper allows greater applications for projects. The jack-in-a-box project on page 142 is a good example of this. Folding can be combined with other techniques such as cutting to create complex patterns such as snowflakes (page 49). When used with sculpting methods it can produce dramatic effects (see page 124). You will find that many of the projects in other chapters of this book also involve folding.

Paper folds best along the grain, rather than against it. To achieve a sharp fold, run a bone folder or the back of a fingernail along the crease. Thicker paper and card will need to be scored first before folding. More information on this technique is provided on page 14, but a few practice scores and folds are necessary to become a skilled papercrafter.

Gliders
Perhaps the most popular of all paper folding projects are the airborne type. As a general rule, the wider the wings, the slower the flight.

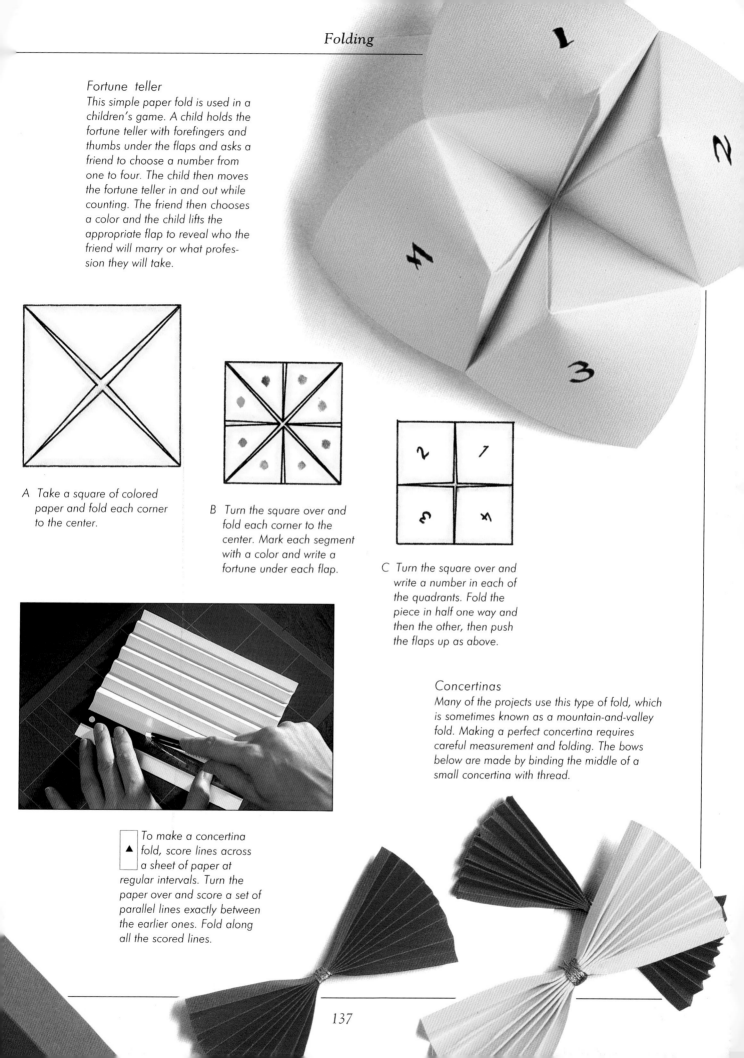

Fortune teller

This simple paper fold is used in a children's game. A child holds the fortune teller with forefingers and thumbs under the flaps and asks a friend to choose a number from one to four. The child then moves the fortune teller in and out while counting. The friend then chooses a color and the child lifts the appropriate flap to reveal who the friend will marry or what profession they will take.

A Take a square of colored paper and fold each corner to the center.

B Turn the square over and fold each corner to the center. Mark each segment with a color and write a fortune under each flap.

C Turn the square over and write a number in each of the quadrants. Fold the piece in half one way and then the other, then push the flaps up as above.

Concertinas

Many of the projects use this type of fold, which is sometimes known as a mountain-and-valley fold. Making a perfect concertina requires careful measurement and folding. The bows below are made by binding the middle of a small concertina with thread.

▲ To make a concertina fold, score lines across a sheet of paper at regular intervals. Turn the paper over and score a set of parallel lines exactly between the earlier ones. Fold along all the scored lines.

PROJECT 46

Concertina File

This colorful file will create order out of chaos when you use it to store all those documents and clippings. As well as color-coding, you could add labels for each of the sections.

YOU WILL NEED
card in several colors
a pencil
a ruler
a knife & mat
a circle template
glue
ribbon
a hole punch

1 Cut eight 16 x 11 " pieces of card in different colors. From one long edge and both short edges, make pencil marks at $^5/_8$ ", $1^1/_4$ " and $1^7/_8$ ". On one face, score the first and third lines, on the reverse, score the middle line. On seven of the sheets, mark and cut a semi-circle on the unscored edge.

2 Cut and score the corners as in the diagram. Dashed lines indicate a score on one face; dotted lines indicate a score on the reverse face. Concertina the sides and base, then fold the corners as shown, tucking and gluing the flaps so they are concealed.

3 Apply glue around the lip of the first section. Place the second section on top, making sure the corners are aligned. Add each of the sections in this way.

4 Cut a $12^1/_4$ x $1^1/_8$ " piece of card and glue it onto the last section of the file. Punch a hole in the two end sections. Cut a length of narrow ribbon and tie a large knot in one end. Thread the ribbon through the holes and tie a bow to close the file.

PROJECT 47

Spills

YOU WILL NEED
brown paper
card
a pencil
a compass
a ruler
glue
scissors
a knife & mat
double-sided tape
ribbon

Spills, or paper twists, were once a basic household item used for lighting fires. These days they are still a good addition to a box of matches and make a quaint decoration for the mantelpiece.

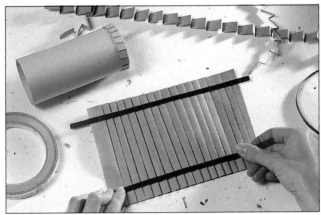

1 Draw a circle with a radius of 1½ " and another inside with a 1¼ " radius. Cut out the larger circle and cut into it to create tabs. Cut a 9 x 5 " rectangle of card and form a cylinder around the disk. Glue the tabs around the outside of the cylinder.

3 Tape over the folds to keep them flat. Trim the piece to fit the cylinder. Apply double-sided tape to a length of ribbon and stick it in two bands over the paper. Wrap this around the cylinder and use the overlapping ribbon to secure it in place.

4 Cut brown paper into rectangles measuring 3 x 8 ". Fold each piece at an angle and twist the end to keep the shape of the spill. Make enough spills to fill the holder.

2 Cut a piece of brown paper 30 x 6 " in size. Score lines across the width at 1½ " intervals. Turn the paper over. Measure ¾ " in from one end and score a line across the width, then at 1½ " intervals. Fold along the score lines so that the paper concertinas.

Suggestion: The box is made from corrugated cardboard rolled in a cylinder, with ends scored and cut into triangles.

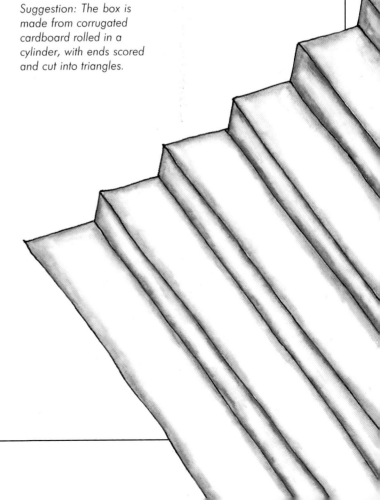

PROJECT 48

Jack-in-a-box

YOU WILL NEED
thick card
colored card
colored paper
acrylic paint
a brush
a knife & mat
glue
a ruler
a pencil
earring wires

The jack in this box is made with techniques borrowed from the ancient art of origami. The spring is folded in a method known to children as Chinese stairs.

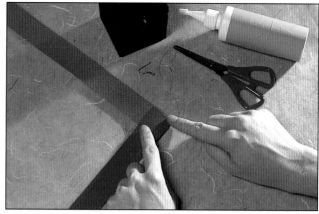

1 On thick card, plot a 2½ " square box (refer to the pattern on page 155 but omit all flaps). Allow a ⅛ " overhang on the lid. Cut and score the box. Glue the sides and base. Cut a 2¼ x 4¾ " strip of card and score it twice to create a 2¼ " square platform which stands 1¼ " high. Paint the box and platform.

2 Attach an earring wire to the box lid. Pierce two holes in the front and insert a wire loop, taping the ends inside. Cut two 1¼ x 28 " strips in different colored card. Glue the ends at right angles and fold one strip over the other repeatedly. Glue the spring onto the platform.

3 Cut a 4½ " square of red paper and fold it as shown. Insert a folded 2¼ " square for the face. Add two folded ⅜ " squares for eyes. Fold the corners of a ¾ x ⅜ " strip and glue it on as a mouth. Glue the face onto the spring so that it fits neatly in the box.

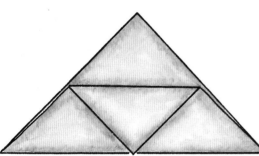

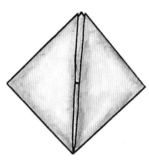

A Fold the square diagonally and fold the top flap down.

B Fold the two lower corners to the top.

C Squash the two corners to create wings.

D Fold half of each wing behind the head.

E Insert the face and fold the points of the hat over.

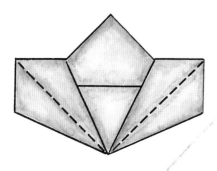

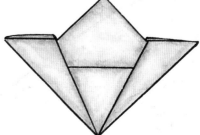

Embossing

The term embossing applies to various methods of changing the surface level of a piece of paper thereby creating an extra dimension. Unlike paper sculpture, it does not involve scoring, folding or bending. Instead, paper can be raised by pressing it over a solid object, or lowered by easing it into a hollow. The degree to which it can be manipulated in this way is limited by the type of paper. The most effective papers are those with a high natural fiber content and which are unglazed. Watercolor paper and hand-made papers are especially suitable.

One necessary item is the block which bears your design; this can be constructed from a range of materials. To create a raised surface, string, rice, dried leaves, wire mesh or similar items can be arranged in place and glued onto a smooth board. The simplest way to form a recessed block is to cut a stencil in card or acetate. For a more complex effect, you can carve a design in linoleum. This allows you to vary the depth, adding a greater degree of subtlety to the embossed design.

Another essential piece of equipment is a blunt tool for burnishing. You can use a variety of household implements, such as the bowl of a teaspoon or the top of a knitting needle. If you plan to do a lot of embossing, it is worthwhile buying an embossing tool from an art supplies store.

The best results will be achieved if you dampen the paper slightly before embossing simply by holding it over a steaming kettle. This stretches the fibers and makes them more pliable. The paper is then laid over the block and burnished. As the burnishing tool often marks the paper, the reverse side is generally more attractive and carries a sharper image.

Embossing is a rewarding technique which can't be hurried. A well-made block can produce multiple works of art and can be used for decorating cards, boxes and stationery, amongst other things.

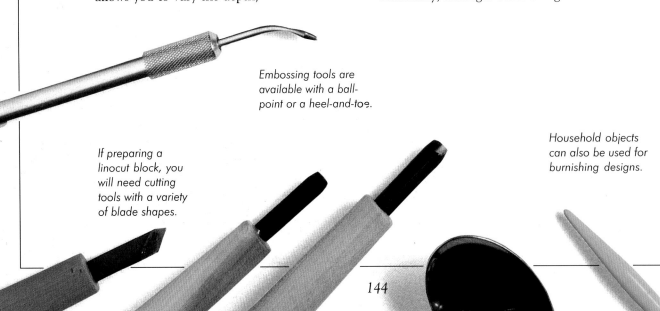

Embossing tools are available with a ball-point or a heel-and-toe.

If preparing a linocut block, you will need cutting tools with a variety of blade shapes.

Household objects can also be used for burnishing designs.

◄ Raised blocks are made by attaching items to a smooth surface. The objects mustn't project too high above the surface or the paper will tear. Paper is placed on top and a blunt tool is used to burnish around the raised areas. Alternatively, a heavy weight can be placed on top, impressing the design into the paper.

◄ Recessed blocks can be made by cutting a stencil in card or by carving a design into a sheet of linoleum. In both methods, the depth should not be too great or the paper will tear. The paper is placed on top of the block and a blunt tool is used to burnish within the hollowed area.

Lighting is important in the display of an embossed piece.

When designing a lowered block, remember to reverse any letters or figures which have a fixed direction.

PROJECT 49

Surprise Boxes

These little boxes are just the right size for a special treat and ideal for those times when the tooth fairy visits. The simple motifs have been embossed using stencil blocks.

YOU WILL NEED

colored card
stiff card
a pencil
tracing paper
a knife & mat
a ruler
an eraser
glue
an embossing tool
a silver or gold pen

1 Cut a 3" square of stiff white card and mark a border ¼" in from each edge. Transfer one of the patterns onto the center of the card and cut out the shape using a sharp knife.

2 Use the pattern on page 155 to mark up a 2½" square box on colored card. Cut out the box shape and score the fold lines. Erase any pencil lines.

Suggestion: Emboss foil over unusual foreign coins, then wrap it around cardboard disks to make magic coins.

3 Lay one face of the box on the stencil so that the inside faces you. Use the guidelines to position it. With an embossing tool, press the card into the stencil, marking the outline firmly. Make sure the card does not move while you work. Repeat for each face of the box.

4 With a gold or silver pen, rule a border on each face of the box. Assemble the box and glue the base tabs. Enclose a small gift.

PROJECT 50

Mirror Frame

The simplest way to emboss paper is over a raised surface. In this project, a wave pattern made with a string block enhances a round mirror or picture.

YOU WILL NEED
thick card
a compass & pencil
a knife & mat
a round mirror
string
white glue
kitchen foil
a thick gold pen
black shoe wax
a stapler
wire

1 ▶ Measure the diameter of your mirror: this is x. From thick card, cut three circles, each with a diameter of x + 4 ". Inside the first, remove another circle with a diameter of x - ¼ "; this ring forms the front of the frame. From the second disk, remove a circle x " in diameter; this ring houses the mirror. The third disk is the backing.

2 ▶ Feed a length of string through a dish of white glue, coating it liberally. Stick the string onto the front piece of the frame in a wavy pattern. Press it down with your fingers.

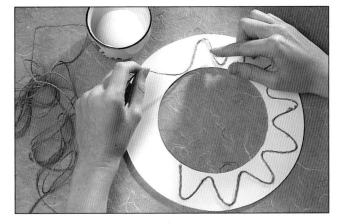

3 ◀ While the glue is still tacky, place a piece of kitchen foil over the string. With clean fingers, mold the foil around the string. Cut the foil in the center and outside edge into spikes which can be turned neatly to the back of the ring.

4 ▶ Color all the edges of the middle and backing disks in gold. Staple a piece of wire to the backing. Smudge liquid shoe wax onto the embossed foil and allow to dry. Glue all three disks together, with the mirror sandwiched tightly in the middle section.

Suggestion: For extra durability, add a coat of acrylic varnish to the frame.

PROJECT 51

Soap Wallet

Subtle shadows cast by the grooves of this embossed shell add a stylish touch to a simple gift. The wallet and the scalloped motif can be adapted to suit the size of the soap.

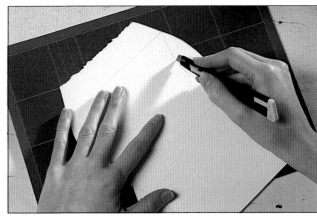

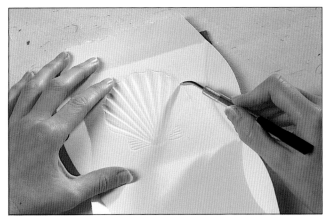

1 Transfer the shell pattern onto a 6 x 4 " piece of linoleum. Cut the outline of the shell with a V-gouge. Use a U-gouge to carefully shape the fan lines: shallow at the base, deeper as they fan out, and shallow again at the edges. Smooth the grooves with the heel of the embossing tool.

2 Enlarge the wallet pattern to 200% and transfer it onto white card. With a craft knife, cut the shape out and score along the dotted lines. Erase any pencil lines. Hold the paper over a steaming kettle to soften the fibers.

3 Turn the wallet so the inside faces you and place it on the linoleum with the lip above the design. Use the foot and heel of the embossing tool to ease the paper into the grooves. Make sure the paper does not move while you work. Glue down the lip and fold the sides.

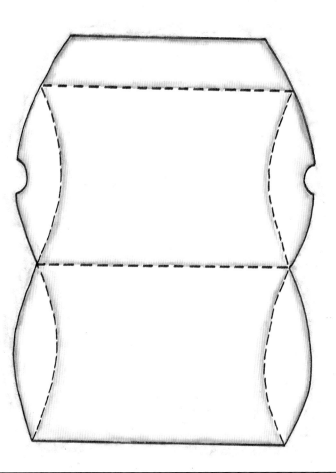

Gift Giving

Few things are more satisfying than giving the right present to a special person. Perhaps one of these is giving the right *handmade* present. You'll find a project in this book to suit people of all age groups and tastes.

Apart from the traditional gift-giving occasions such as birthdays and Christmas, there are plenty of times throughout the year when papercraft gifts would be welcomed and treasured for a long time.

Someone celebrating the arrival of a baby would appreciate the baby kit (Project 43) or the picture frame (Project 17). For friends setting up a new home, choose from any of the projects marked with a house motif.

Halloween is a time for children, and surprise boxes full of sweets (Project 49) would make an ideal treat.

Wish a friend bon voyage with a gift of handmade stationery (Project 7) or an embossed soap wallet (Project 51).

Traditionally, a first wedding anniversary is marked with a gift of paper, so anything from this book would be suitable!

You don't need any excuse to make a gift of flowers. Paper flowers can be made in different shapes and textures: some can even be sent in the post. See the index for the flower projects in this book.

Even if your gift isn't made of paper, you can add a stylish touch with paper accessories. Tassels, fans and bows are just some of the paper items which take only a moment to make but can transform a plain parcel into a delightful gift.

Simple bud roses can be made by rolling strips of twisted paper ribbon. These can then be glued onto cards or presents.

Instructions for making crêpe paper roses appear on page 127.

1 ▶ To make paper tassels, cut a 6 x 3 " piece of paper and fold it into a square. With a sharp knife and a metal ruler, cut a series of lines from ½ " below the folded edge to the bottom.

2 ◀ Tape one end of a gold thread to the top edge of the paper. Roll the paper tightly and then bind the tassel with the gold thread. Use a needle to pull the thread under the binding and pull it tight. The thread can then be used to attach the tassel to a gift.

Beautiful bows
Use twist ribbon to create old-fashioned bows. The best effect is gained by cutting separate pieces and assembling them as shown.

Making Boxes

There are always times when you need a box of a specific size and shape. Indeed, many of the projects in this book will require one, especially if you plan to give them as gifts. There is no great secret to making boxes, just a bit of planning and some careful cutting and scoring.

Choose a stiff card, strong enough for the purpose. For large boxes you will need to use board, which is thick enough for two pieces to be glued end to end. Boxes made from thinner card will need tabs or flaps to secure the edges. Before you start to make a new type of box, it is worthwhile making one up in paper first. This allows you to check that all the angles and dimensions are correct before cutting more expensive card to shape.

Boxes needn't be square or rectangular. Experiment with different shapes to see what can be achieved. Add interest to regular shaped boxes by decorating them with such papercraft techniques as quilling, stenciling or froissage. Old boxes which once held chocolates or perfume can be given a new life by covering them with giftwrap or self-adhesive plastic.

▶ *Foil-covered and corrugated card make interesting boxes. You will find the pattern for the wallet on page 151. Boxes with attached lids are easy to make: a basic pattern for a square box is given on the next page.*

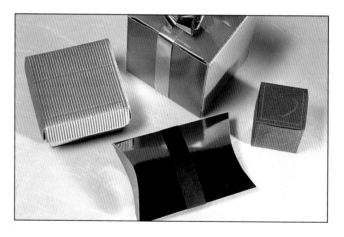

◀ *Boxes with fitted lids require careful measurement as the base should be slightly smaller than the lid. Oval boxes are made using the same method as round ones (see the instructions on the next page).*

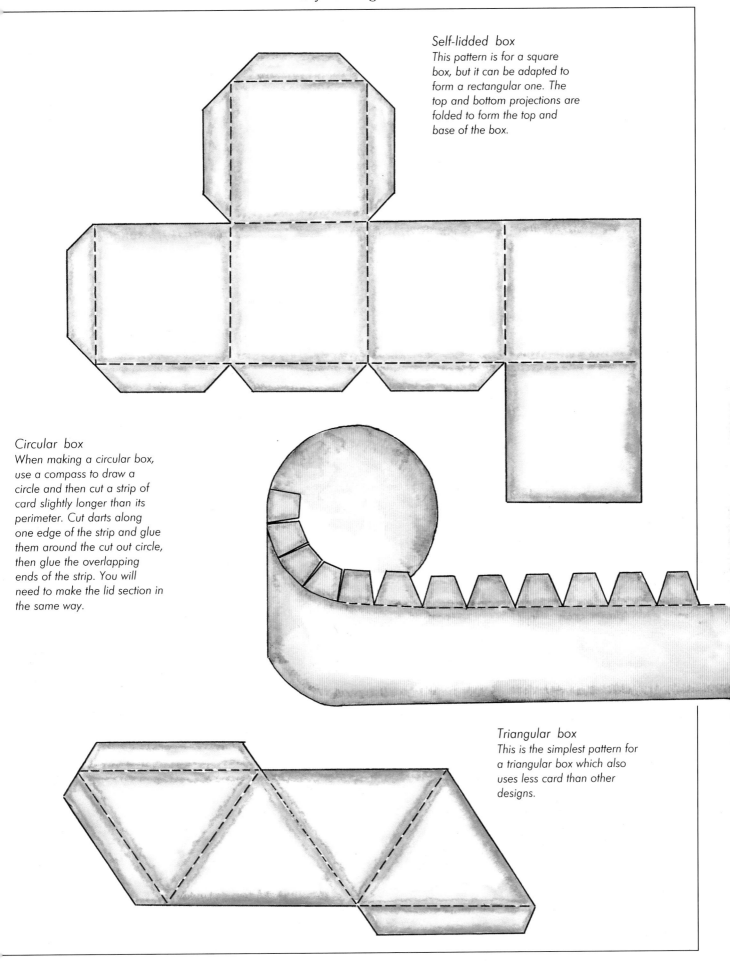

Self-lidded box
This pattern is for a square box, but it can be adapted to form a rectangular one. The top and bottom projections are folded to form the top and base of the box.

Circular box
When making a circular box, use a compass to draw a circle and then cut a strip of card slightly longer than its perimeter. Cut darts along one edge of the strip and glue them around the cut out circle, then glue the overlapping ends of the strip. You will need to make the lid section in the same way.

Triangular box
This is the simplest pattern for a triangular box which also uses less card than other designs.

Wrapping Presents

The art of wrapping is part of the tradition of gift-giving. How well a present is wrapped says something about the spirit in which it is given. Elaborate decoration is unnecessary, but neat folds and a thoughtful presentation make a world of difference.

These days, there are many lovely commercial giftwraps available. So many, in fact, that the array can be quite overwhelming. You might consider using plain brown paper and creating a more natural effect.

For an inexpensive and more personalised giftwrap, try making your own. No matter what the result, you will have fun and your friends will appreciate your efforts. Buy a large roll of light, unsized paper and decorate it with a simple repeat pattern by stenciling or printing. Medium-sized sheets of paper can also be marbled. If you need to make a large quantity, the oil-on-water method is the quickest.

Giftwrap ribbon or the narrower curling ribbon is ideal for adorning a plain parcel. If your paper is heavily patterned, you may find that a ribbon is unnecessary.

Awkwardly shaped presents might be best presented in a box or attractive bag. For details on making boxes, see pages 154-155. Instructions for making gift bags are to be found on the next page.

1 ▶ To make a gift bag, plan the size required and draw a pattern on paper as shown. Cut out the shape and score the base flaps and the sides. For a more shaped bag, turn the paper over and score a center line down each side panel. Fold the bag into shape.

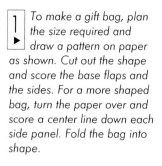

2 ◀ Glue the side flap. On the base, glue the short flaps onto one long flap and glue the other long flap onto that. Punch two holes on either side at the top of the bag. Attach ribbon or string to form handles.

Paste paper
Wrapping paper is fun and easy to make. Thicken acrylic paint with wallpaper paste. Sponge it lightly onto a sheet of paper, or brush it on thickly and then create patterns with a comb-shaped piece of thick card.

Making Tags & Cards

Gift tags don't just serve to sort out the jumble of presents under the Christmas tree: they can also enhance the gift wrapping. The best tags are co-ordinated with the wrapping paper; if you've bought giftwrap you could découpage a motif from it onto the tag. Unlike cards, which are expected to stand upright, tags can be cut in any shape to match the occasion.

Greeting cards can be created using any of the techniques in this book. If you plan to send them through the post, quilling or sculpting a card is less practical but dimen-

sion can be created with a pop-up or embossed design. Most cards are single folds with an upright or "portrait" format, but only by tradition. You might add interest with a concertina fold or a gate fold, which opens like french windows. To frame another piece of paper in a card you can make a three-panel mount as shown on the next page.

Some techniques such as printing, stenciling and marbling are particularly suitable for making multiple cards as well as wrapping paper. Handmade paper can be used to make beautiful cards, even when unadorned.

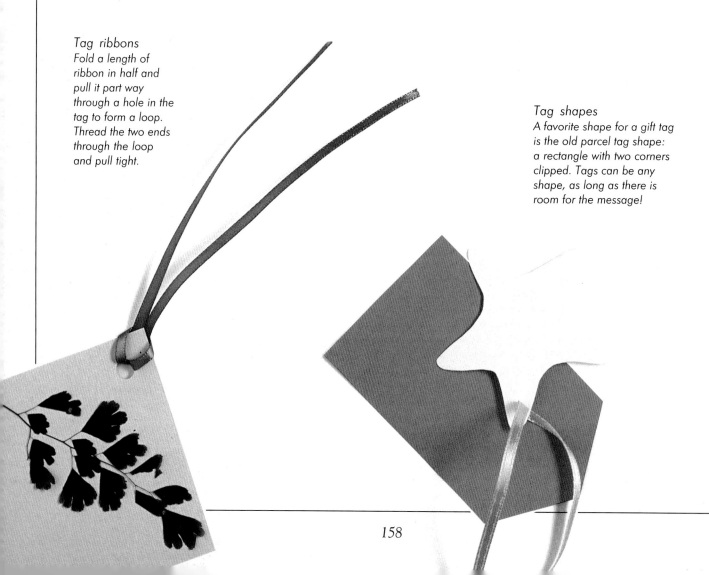

Tag ribbons
Fold a length of ribbon in half and pull it part way through a hole in the tag to form a loop. Thread the two ends through the loop and pull tight.

Tag shapes
A favorite shape for a gift tag is the old parcel tag shape: a rectangle with two corners clipped. Tags can be any shape, as long as there is room for the message!

While you are making a papercraft gift, make a matching tag. Unlike cards, which are often given in an envelope, tags do not need to be perfectly flat so embossing, quilling and dimensionals are all viable decorating techniques.

Make a batch of greeting cards rather than just one at a time. This way, you'll have a supply of handmade cards for any occasion that arises.

Three-panel mounts
To frame a work in a card, score a piece of card into three equal sections. Cut a window in the middle panel. Trim a strip off the left edge. Mount the work so that it can be viewed through the window, then fold and stick down the narrow panel.

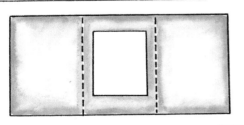

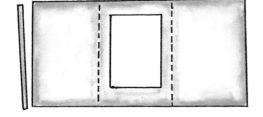

Index

Acknowledgments & Sources

Thanks are due to Lynne Cunningham who devised the three projects in the dimensionals chapter and to Betty and Charles Marsh for general assistance.
The publisher would also like to thank the following for materials and items which appear in this book:
Project 11 - pictures are from *William Tell*, by Margaret Early and published by Walter McVitty.

Projects 16, 17 © Paper Tole Creations & Supplies Pty. Ltd. 1994. Kits for these and for Project 18 are available from Lynne's Paper Tole Creations & Supplies, 3/18 Laser Drive, Rowville, Victoria 3178, Australia. Overseas enquiries are welcome.
Page 96 - marbled papers are by Il Papiro of Florence, Italy.